T

MW00437293

THE SPIRIT AND
THE CHURCH

Abridged and made easy to read by
R.J.K. Law

THE BANNER OF TRUTH TRUST

THE BANNER OF TRUTH TRUST

Head Office
3 Murrayfield Road
Edinburgh
EH12 6EL
UK

North America Office
PO Box 621
Carlisle
PA 17013
USA

banneroftruth.org

*

ISBN
978 0 85151 822 0

*

Typeset in 10.5/12.5 Baskerville MT
at The Banner of Truth Trust, Edinburgh

Printed in the USA by
Versa Press Inc.,
East Peoria, IL.

*

Scripture quotations are taken from the New King James Version
© 1983 by Thomas Nelson, Inc.

Publisher's Preface

The Puritan era in seventeenth-century England was distinguished most of all by its school of evangelical authors whose writings have had such a powerful influence wherever they have been read. Among these men none has been regarded more highly than John Owen, whose works combine biblical insight and theology with spirituality and experimental religion to such a marked degree. As an indication of the value placed upon him by the present publishers it may be noted that the sixteen volumes of his *Works* (in the Goold edition of 1850–53) have been kept in print ever since they were first reprinted in 1965 on account of their importance, and the seven volumes of his exposition of *Hebrews* have been available since 1991. We hope that the availability of the full text of Owen can be continued; the abridgements which are now being issued are not meant as a replacement.

Those who have accused Owen of being hard to read have generally been people who lacked the time to read him as he deserves. But considering the extent of his writings even those who wish to read him more fully have often, for the same reason, been unable to become as familiar with him as they would wish. Many cannot read enough to be able to determine which of his books contain his finest work and there can be few alive who have read all of his *Works*. As a result many of Owen's most important and relevant treatises are little known today. The Rev. R.J.K. Law, the abridger of this text, began his work purely for his own profit and as a memory aid. As he proceeded, he felt more and more like the men of 2 Kings chapter seven who, discovering the riches of the deserted camp of the Syrians, exclaimed, 'This day is a day of good tidings, and we hold our peace.' The desire that others should share in his findings thus led to a change in his original purpose.

On examining the quality of Dr Law's abridgements we have fully shared his enthusiasm for putting the best of Owen into the hands of as many readers as possible.

The 'discourses' (to use Owen's term) in this book are all from volume 4 of the 16-volume set referred to above. They should be considered as completing what was begun in the abridgement of volume 3, published in the Puritan Paperback series in 1998 as *The Holy Spirit* (ISBN 978 0 85151 698 1, 216 pp.). In Owen's words, they concern 'the work of the Holy Spirit as the Spirit of illumination, of supplication, of consolation and as the immediate author of all spiritual offices and gifts'. This material is vitally important for the well-being of the church today. Parts 1 and 2, on the work of the Spirit in illuminating our minds as to the nature and contents of Scripture, remain as important as when first written, in view of modern views which subordinate Scripture to the Spirit and exalt the 'inner light'. The other discourses are also richly enlightening as to the nature of prayer, spiritual comfort and spiritual gifts, and the work of the Spirit in these. Throughout, the balance Owen maintains between the Word and the Spirit, not over- or understating the rôle of either, is impressive.

The Bible version used throughout is the *New King James Version*. For maximum benefit, the reader should look up the Scripture verses cited and consider them in relation to the points Owen is making, with fervent prayer for the grace and help of the Holy Spirit.

Contents

Publisher's Preface   v

PART ONE: *How We Believe Scripture to Be
the Word of God*
1. Illumination Based on Revelation   1
2. The Faith by Which We Believe Scripture
to Be God's Word   7
3. External Arguments for Divine Revelation   10
4. Moral Certainty, the Result of External
Arguments, Insufficient   14
5. Divine Revelation Itself the Only Foundation
and Reason for Faith   26
6. The Self-Evidencing Power of Scripture   33
7. The Kind of Assurance Scripture Brings   42

Part Two: *Understanding the Mind of God*
1. How We Learn the Mind of God from
Scripture   49
2. Knowing the Mind of God: Some Teaching
from Scripture Itself   52
3. How Are Believers Guided into 'All Truth'?   58
4. How Does the Holy Spirit Enlighten Our
Minds?   64
5. Hindrances to the Understanding of the
Mind of God in Scripture   68
6. The Nature of Scripture, and the Right
Approach to It   72

  7. Means to be Used to Understand the
     Mind of God in Scripture   77
  8. Tools from Various Disciplines to Aid in
     Our Understanding of Scripture   79
  9. Help from the Church to Understand
     Scripture   81
 10. Final Points on the Work of the Spirit
     in Relation to Scripture   84

PART THREE: *The Holy Spirit and Prayer*
  1. The Help of the Spirit in Prayer   89
  2. The Spirit of Grace and Supplication:
     Zechariah 12:10 Expounded   91
  3. The Spirit of Adoption: Galatians 4:6
     Expounded   97
  4. The Nature of Prayer: Romans 8:26
     Vindicated   100
  5. The Spirit Teaches Us What to Pray For   102
  6. The Spirit Teaches Us How to Pray   108
  7. The Duty of Praying in the Spirit:
     Ephesians 6:18 Expounded   113
  8. The Spirit Enables Us to Pray Aloud   117
  9. Our Response to the Gift of the Spirit
     of Prayer   123
 10. Contemplative Prayer Considered   130
 11. Set Forms of Prayer Examined   137

PART FOUR: *The Holy Spirit as a Comforter*
  1. How the Spirit Comforts the Church   143
  2. The Characteristics of the Spirit's Work
     as Comforter   148

3. The Holy Spirit Comforts Only Believers ... 153
4. The Indwelling of the Holy Spirit ... 155
5. The Holy Spirit as an Anointing ... 160
6. The Holy Spirit Seals Believers ... 164
7. The Holy Spirit as an Earnest or Guarantee ... 168

PART FIVE: *The Gifts of the Holy Spirit*
1. The Purpose of Spiritual Gifts ... 171
2. Spiritual Gifts and Saving Grace ... 173
3. The Extraordinary Offices of the Church ... 178
4. Extraordinary Spiritual Gifts in the Church ... 180
5. How Spiritual Gifts Promote Christ's Kingdom ... 184
6. The Continuance of the Ministry ... 187
7. Spiritual Gifts Granted to the Ministry ... 189
8. The Gifts of the Spirit for Doctrine, Worship and Discipline ... 192

Part One

How We Believe Scripture to Be the Word of God

1: Illumination Based on Revelation

The work of the Holy Spirit in the illumination or enlightening of the minds of men is the main subject of the discourse on the Holy Spirit of which this is a part. This work of illumination is distinctly described in Scripture (*Eph.* 1:17, 18; *Heb.* 6:4; *Luke* 2:32; *Acts* 13:47; 16:14; 26:18; *2 Cor.* 4:4; *1 Pet.* 2:9).

The outward means that this illumination is founded on, the Scripture, is the principal topic we will consider in the present discussion, giving particular attention to this question: *What is the basis of our believing the Scripture to be the Word of God, with that divine and supernatural faith which is required of us by God, and which it is our duty to give?*

ILLUMINATION AND REVELATION

What then is 'illumination'? Illumination is the effect of a divine work wrought in the minds of men enabling them to know the mind and will of God, as supernaturally revealed to them, as the law or rule of their faith, life and obedience.

Supernatural *revelation* is the basis of supernatural *illumination*. These things go together. There is a natural knowledge of supernatural things, which is both theoretical and practical (*Rom.* 1:19 and 2:14–15). And there may be a supernatural knowledge of natural things, as when God gave supernatural wisdom about natural things to

Solomon (*1 Kings* 4:31–34). God also gave Bezalel supernatural wisdom to enable him to build the tabernacle (*Exod.* 31:2–6). Without this, both Solomon and Bezalel would have had to spend years gaining that knowledge which God gave them supernaturally.

But *supernatural illumination* relates to what has been *supernaturally revealed* and is wrought in us by the immediate power of the Spirit of God (*1 Cor.* 2:9–10; *Eph.* 1:17–19; *2 Cor.* 4:6). David prayed for this illumination (*Psa.* 119:18). 'Open', 'reveal', or 'uncover my eyes', bring light and understanding into my mind, 'that I may see wondrous things from Your law.' As if to say, 'Uncover my eyes that I may see with unveiled face', or as in the Syriac, 'with a revealed or uncovered face', 'wondrous things from Your law'. He prayed for inward light, the illumination or enlightening of the mind. The light he prayed for had to do only with the outward doctrine of the law. The writer to the Hebrews declares the nature of God's outward revelations (*Heb.* 1:1–2). The various supernatural revelations that he has made of himself, his mind and will, from first to last, are the sole foundation on which the supernatural illumination we are speaking of rests.

This divine external revelation was given by God 'at various times and in various ways'(*Heb.* 1:1). It came with its own supernatural evidence that it was from God, and this was sufficient to convince the minds of those who received it. When it was preached to others by those who had received it directly from God, a divine power infallibly assured the hearers that the revelation came from God, so that they were able to resist Satanic delusions, claiming to be divine revelations, preached by false prophets at that time. These evidences accompanying divine revelations were particularly directed to faith, as the Scriptures are, and not to the outward senses.

[2]

The evidence we are talking about is not like the sun which proves its own existence by the light that shines from it. We can see it clearly and do not have to assure ourselves by reasoning that it exists. But it is like the evidence that the heavens and the earth give of their being created by the power of God. While they give this evidence undeniably and infallibly (*Psa.* 19:1, 2; *Rom.* 1:19–21), yet we are still required to use our reasoning ability to come to the right conclusion as we consider and meditate on them. Where men fail to do this, notwithstanding the clear evidence they have of God's majesty and glory, they degenerate into atheism.

In all his revelations God required men to exercise faith, conscience, obedience and reason towards them. When they did this, they received full assurance that the revelation came from God. God's Word differs from all else that claims to be revelation as the wheat does from the chaff (*Jer.* 23:8). But it is our duty to try to sift the wheat from the chaff.

The revelations which God gave were sufficient to guide and direct all to whom they came in the knowledge of their duty to God. They clearly showed man what God required of him, in the way of faith and obedience.

Each generation had enough light to guide them in faith and obedience. Men had enough knowledge to offer sacrifices in faith as did Abel, enough knowledge to walk with God as did Enoch, and enough knowledge to teach their families the fear of the Lord, as did Abraham. Enoch was given sufficient revelation to prophesy, warn and instruct others (*Jude* 14–15). Noah had sufficient revelation to become a preacher of righteousness (*2 Pet.* 2:5). Abraham was given sufficient revelation to command his children and household to keep the way of the Lord (*Gen.* 18:19).

[3]

OLD AND NEW TESTAMENT REVELATION

Yet these revelations were 'as a light shining in a dark place'. The Old Testament was like a candle in a dark room, or like the stars and the moon on a dark night. When the sun rises, there is no longer any use for the candle, and the moon and the stars fade into insignificance. So when the full glory of the gospel rose and the Sun of righteousness came, the Old Testament types and ceremonies were no longer needed. As we study them, we may yet see the light that was in them, though it is now to us as a candle shining in full daylight.

There was also in the Old Testament a sufficient ministry for the declaration of the revelations which God made of himself and his will. There was the natural ministry of parents who were obliged to instruct their children in the knowledge of the truth which they had received. There was also the extraordinary ministry of those whom God entrusted with new revelations of himself, both to confirm and to give further light on the earlier revelations they had received, even before any divine revelations were recorded in writing.

INSUFFICIENCY OF UNWRITTEN REVELATION

However, this way of teaching was imperfect and insufficient to retain the knowledge of God in the world. Under this dispensation the generality of men fell into great apostasy from God. So God suffered all nations to walk in their own ways and gave them up to their own hearts' lusts to walk in their own counsels (*Acts* 14:16; *Psa.* 81:12). This was because of their wickedness and base ingratitude, but happened all the more easily because there was no certain standard of truth to which men might go. It may be said that since the revelation of the will of God has been committed to writing, men have still apostatized from the knowledge of God. I answer that this has not come about by any defect in the way and means of illumination, nor in the way in which God gave his truth to men, but because of men's wickedness and ingratitude. God has justly given them up to destruction (*Rom.* 1:18; *2 Thess.* 2:11, 12; *Luke* 13:3).

But now God has gathered up into Scripture all divine revelations given by himself from the beginning of the world, and all that ever shall be to the end of the world, for the general use of the church. This is so that we might be thoroughly instructed in the mind and will of God, be guided aright in worship and obedience here, and be brought to eternal joy hereafter.

When God gave the law and committed it to writing, he forbade any to add to it (*Deut.* 4:2; 12:32). All further revelations given to the church under the Old Testament were gathered in writing in the later books. When the full revelation of the whole mind of God, to which nothing is ever to be added, was perfected by Jesus Christ, all was by divine inspiration committed to writing (*Heb.* 1:1, 2; *Luke* 1:4; *Acts* 1:1; *John* 20:31).

As the Old Testament closed with a warning, so also the New Testament concludes with a warning to any who should presume to add anything more (*Mal.* 4:4-6; *Rev.* 22:18).

Therefore, *Scripture is now the only external means of divine spiritual illumination*, because it is the only repository of all divine supernatural revelation (*Psa.* 19:7, 8; *Isa.* 8:20; *2 Tim.* 3:15–17).

In asserting this, we are not excluding all those subordinate means which God has given to make it do its work effectively in our hearts and souls. We must, of course, read, study and meditate on those things given to us in Scripture (*Deut.* 6:6, 7; 11:18; *Josh.* 1:18; *Psa.* 1:2; 119; *Col.* 3:16; *2 Tim.* 3:15). Bread will nourish no-one who does not obtain it and feed on it.

The mutual instruction of one another out of the Scriptures is also required, so that we may communicate to each other the knowledge of the mind of God (*Deut.* 6:7; *Luke* 24:26, 27, 32).

The ministry of the Word in the church is another important means of making known the mind and will of God (*Matt.* 5:14, 15; *2 Cor.* 5:18–20; *Eph.* 4:11-15; *1 Tim.* 3:15).

Now, for Scripture, which contains the whole of divine revelation, to be a sufficient external means of illumination to us, we must first *believe* it to be a divine revelation (*2 Pet.* 1:19-21; *Heb.* 1:1; *2 Tim.* 3:16; *Isa.* 8:20; *1 Thess.* 2:13; *Neh.* 8:8; *Isa.* 28:9; *Hos.* 14:9; *Prov.* 1:6; *Psa.* 119:34; *Matt.* 15:16; *2 Tim.* 2:7; *1 John* 5:20). Secondly, we must *understand* the things contained in Scripture (*Isa.* 29: 11, 12; *Psa.* 119:30; *Luke* 24:27, 45; *Acts* 8:31, 34, 35). The first of these is the subject of Part 1 of this book. The latter is the subject of Part 2.

Both of these are to be considered as part of the illumination which is accomplished in us by the Spirit. What I shall affirm in the following discussion is that *it is the work of the Holy Spirit to enable us to believe Scripture to be the Word of God, and infallibly to evidence it to be so to our minds, so that we spiritually and savingly rest in it.*

By this I do not mean, as some assume, that faith in Scripture comes from a private, personal revelation given to each person by the Spirit, or any self-deluding claim of that kind, nor do I exclude all rational arguments and external testimonies to Scripture as the Word of God.

Indeed we affirm nothing on this subject but what the church, ancient and modern, has always believed.

2: The Faith by Which We Believe Scripture to Be God's Word

We are considering what it is to believe with a faith which cannot be mistaken that the Scripture is the Word of God, and the basis of our doing so. After that, we will consider the fact that there are also external arguments for the divine origin of the Scripture.

As to our believing, two things are to be considered: *what it is that we believe,* and *the reason why we believe it.*

We believe all that is revealed and declared to us in Scripture, and we believe it *because* it is revealed there, not for any external reason (*1 Cor.* 15:3, 4; *Acts* 8:28–38; 26:22, 23, 27; *John* 2:22).

The faith by which we believe Scripture to be the Word of God is not any kind of faith or persuasion, but that which is *divine and infallible.* It must be so because what causes it and what it is based on is divine and infallible. As in the case of the Samaritans, our faith may begin with the testimony of men, but it must progress to that which is of God and therefore cannot be mistaken (*John* 4:40–42).

When we speak of faith that is infallible we are not referring to some inherent quality in the person who believes, as if he were infallible. What we are saying is that the assent our minds give to divine truths or supernatural revelations is different from every other kind of assent, and this is because the evidence on which it is based is from God and is infallible.

That the Scripture is the Word of God is infallibly true, but men may believe this for a fallible reason, from tradition, or on the testimony of the church only, or from outward arguments. This leads only to a natural, human faith. For the kind of faith we are speaking of, it is not enough that the thing believed is infallibly true. There also has to be infallible evidence that it is so, on the basis of which we believe. Then our faith is infallible, though we ourselves are fallible.

This was the case with those who received divine revelations immediately from God. It was not enough that the things revealed were infallibly true. Those who received them also had to have infallible evidence of the revelation itself. Then their faith was infallible, though they were fallible. With this kind of faith a man can believe nothing but what is divinely true. The truthfulness of God – the God of truth (*Deut.* 32:4) – is the only foundation on which it rests. That faith which is in God and his Word is *fixed on truth*, or is infallible (*2 Chron.* 20:20).

This faith therefore rests only on the authority and truthfulness of God, who has spoken in Scripture (*Deut.* 32:4; *Titus* 1:2; *John* 17:17; *1 John* 5:6).

FAITH SUPERNATURAL, INFALLIBLE AND DIVINE

Our faith is supernatural because it is produced in our minds by the Holy Spirit. It is infallible because the only thing it rests on is infallible divine revelation. And it is divine, as opposed to what is merely human, for both reasons. Such faith leads to loving obedience and submission to God's mind and will as these are made known (*2 Sam.* 7:28; *Isa.* 30:15; 57:15; *2 Chron.* 20:20).

The only way we can rest on the truth and veracity of God in anything is to rest on the revelation which he has made to us, for that is the only way in which our minds and consciences are affected by these things. 'The Lord is true' is a proposition to which our minds assent. But what immediately affects us is when we hear 'Thus says the Lord', and 'the Lord has spoken'.

[8]

These alone affect our minds with the authority and veracity of God, however they are made known to us. And now all revelation is contained in the Scripture alone. So it is on Scripture alone that our faith rests.

But how, or on what grounds, or for what reasons, do we believe Scripture to be a divine revelation, proceeding directly from God? I answer: *We believe it solely on the evidence that the Spirit of God, in and by Scripture itself, gives to us that it was indeed given by the immediate inspiration of God; or, the basis of our believing the Scripture to be the Word of God is the evidence we find there of the authority and truth of God making themselves known to the minds and consciences of men.* So we believe the Scripture to be the Word of God on no other grounds than *its own evidence that it is indeed so.*

This is what we intend to prove in what follows, but first we must speak of the external arguments for the Scriptures as a revelation from God.

3: External Arguments for Divine Revelation

There are convincing external arguments for the reality of divine revelation. They cannot be the basis of a faith which is divine and supernatural, but they are useful to confirm our faith against temptations, oppositions and objections. Those external arguments which seem most forceful to me include these:

1. THE ANTIQUITY OF THESE WRITINGS

What is most ancient is most true. God himself makes use of this argument against idols. The true God was among his people before any strange god was known or named (*Isa.* 43:10–12). In a similar way, Scripture was in the world long before any other thing or writing claiming to be a revelation from God, as can be shown from history.

2. THE PRESERVATION OF SCRIPTURE

God preserved his Word all through the Babylonish captivity, then under the Persian monarchy. Under the Grecian monarchy, an attempt was made to destroy the Scriptures utterly, but to no avail. The Romans destroyed Jerusalem and the temple and carried away the ancient copy of the law to Rome. They also endeavoured to destroy the Holy Scriptures. But all their attempts failed (*Matt.* 5:18).

The anti-Christian church which rose up in the world was built on men's opinions and traditions which were false. Yet this wicked church did not dare to alter one line of Scripture, instead adding to it its own traditions.

All this proves the watchful care and power of divine providence in the preservation of God's holy Word.

3. THE SCOPE OF THESE WRITINGS

All Scripture and all its parts have the stamp of divine wisdom and authority upon them, with respect to two purposes: to reveal God to man, and to direct men to the eternal enjoyment of God.

Scripture speaks in the name and authority of God and says nothing and commands nothing but that which agrees with his infinite holiness, wisdom and goodness. In addition, Scripture alone teaches men how to live to God, and how to come to that perfect enjoyment of God.

4. THE TESTIMONY OF THE CHURCH

The church testifies that Scripture is the divine revelation of God. The church is said to be the pillar and ground of the truth (*1 Tim.* 3:15) because it testifies to the truth of Scripture. But here we must distinguish between the sense in which the testimony of the church is of weight and the false interpretation which the church of Rome has put on this. We deny that the authority of Scripture is dependent on the testimony of the church, as Rome would have us believe. Far from receiving its authority from the church, the church only has authority insofar as it is based on Scripture. Nevertheless, it is the church's duty and ministry to declare that Scripture is the infallible Word of God.

The testimony that is of weight in this matter is that of multitudes of persons of unspotted reputation in the world, free from the possibility of being accused of planning evil or making a conspiracy among themselves, persons who sought no secular or worldly advantage by their testimony.

This includes the testimony of those who wrote Scripture. They all claimed that what they wrote was received by direct inspiration from God (*2 Pet.* 1:16–21). As to their persons, they were above suspicion of deceiving or being deceived. They generally had nothing to gain and everything to lose by their testimony. Their style or manner of writing also deserves special consideration. Everything here is consistent with their affirmation that what they wrote was from God and was given by divine inspiration.

We have also the testimony of all those who have believed in Christ through their word (*John* 17:20). These also testified that Scripture was good, holy and true in all its contents, and that the whole and every part of it was given by divine inspiration (*2 Pet.* 1:20–21).

The testimony was sometimes given by miraculous works (*Heb.* 2:4; *Acts* 5:32). It was often given through men's sufferings (*Acts* 22:20; *Rev.* 2:13: 17:6). Generally it was given by all of their lives, in all that they thought, spoke and did.

The tremendous success of the gospel in the world against all worldly opposition, considering who they were who brought the gospel to the world and how they brought it, shows Scripture to be God's Word. Some of the apostles and evangelists were fishermen, poor, lowly, despised. They brought the gospel to the world by the foolishness of preaching Christ crucified. This doctrine of Christ crucified was a stumbling block to the Jews and foolishness to the Greeks.

The gospel was first preached at a time of peace, prosperity and plenty. To receive it demanded renunciation of the world, the cutting off of the right hand and the plucking out of the right eye.

It may be objected that we do not now see the gospel as successful as it was in its first days. Therefore, either it was pure chance that made it successful, or we have another gospel today which is not the gospel of God.

We answer, the gospel is the same as ever it was from the beginning. The major cause of its present lack of success lies in the sovereign will and pleasure of God. It is also the case that many nations have held the truth in unrighteousness, provoking God to remove the gospel from them.

All these arguments might be stated at length. Yet, however strong and convincing the external arguments may be, they cannot lead to our believing the Scriptures to be the Word of God with that faith which is infallible, supernatural and divine.

CONCLUSION

Where the things to be believed are divine and supernatural, so must the faith be by which we believe them or give assent to them. Although the external arguments by which learned men have proved, or may yet further prove, Scripture to be a divine revelation are useful to strengthen the faith of those who believe and to convince opposers, to say that our faith is the effect and product of them and rests upon them is contrary to Scripture, overthrows the nature of true faith, and excludes the work of the Holy Spirit in the whole matter.

4: Moral Certainty, the Result of External Arguments, Insufficient

Divine revelation is the proper object of divine faith. Divine faith cannot believe that anything is divine revelation except that which truly is (*1 Cor.* 2:4, 5, 13; 14:36–37; *2 Cor.* 4:7). If we do not believe Scripture with a divine faith, we do not believe Scripture to be truly of God. That 'Scripture is the Word of God' is a divine revelation and so it is to be believed. But God does not require us to believe this on human testimony or by human reasoning, but on his divine authority and truthfulness. 'I am the Lord.' 'To the law and to the testimony.' 'This is my beloved Son, hear him!' 'All Scripture is given by inspiration of God.' 'Believe the Lord and his prophets.' We only believe Scripture to be God's Word with a divine faith when we believe it on the testimony of God's authority alone.

When God gave the Ten Commandments, he gave us no other reason why we should obey them than this only, 'I am the Lord your God'. The reason we obey God is that he is our God and we are his people. Nor does God give us any other reason why we should believe him, or why we should believe the revelation he has given us of his mind and will. Our faith is the root and chief part of our obedience. Our obedience to his commandments and our faith in his revelation are both based on his divine authority and truthfulness.

Neither our Lord Jesus Christ nor his apostles ever made use of human arguments and reasons to bring people to believe the gospel they preached. But when they were accused of following 'cunningly devised fables', they appealed to Moses and the prophets, to the revelations they themselves had received, and to those revelations that had been written before in the Scriptures. It is true that they wrought miracles which confirmed and established their divine mission and the doctrine they taught, but the miracles of our Saviour were all of them wrought among those who believed the whole of Scripture, then given, to be the Word of God. And the miracles performed by the apostles were done before the New Testament books were written.

Their doctrine, therefore, and their authority to teach it were abundantly confirmed by the miracles But divine revelation itself, both as originally given and as written, was left to be received by faith on the authority of God alone. The apostles did not appeal to human reason or arguments to persuade people to believe. In fact they decried such means as unprofitable, and appealed only to the authority of God working with power in and by his Word preached. In proof of this, consider again the verses given at the beginning of this chapter.

The sum of what we are saying is this: *We are obliged to believe the Scriptures to be a divine revelation solely because of the authority and truthfulness of God speaking in them.* We believe them because they are the Word of God. This faith is divine and supernatural because what it is based on is divine and supernatural, that is, God's truthfulness and authority manifested there.

Therefore we ought not to believe that it is only highly probable that Scripture is God's Word, nor because we have been persuaded by human reason or argument, which are fallible. We believe Scripture to be God's Word because of God's truth and authority seen there. This is divine, supernatural faith. And without divine, supernatural faith, we do not truly believe at all.

[15]

MORAL CERTAINTY DISTINGUISHED FROM FAITH

Moral certainty is the result of mere persuasion or human reason. If we were required to believe only on human testimony or by human reason and persuasion, then there would be no need of any work of the Holy Spirit to enable us to believe or to work faith in us. But in Scripture we read that faith is 'the gift of God' and is 'not of ourselves' (*Eph.* 2:8). It is 'given [to some] on the behalf of Christ' (*Phil.* 1:29; *Matt.* 11:25; 13:11). But faith based on human reason or testimony is based on ourselves and is possible for all to come to on these grounds.

'No man can say that Jesus is Lord, except by the Holy Spirit' (*1 Cor.* 12:3). But he who believes the Scripture to be true on the authority of God, as is his duty to do, does say 'Jesus is Lord'. No man comes to Christ, but he that has 'heard and learned of the Father' (*John* 6:45). But if we can come to Christ by moral persuasion and by human testimony, what need is there to be taught by the Father?

All human arguments are fallible, because they are human. They are based on men's opinions only, and the highest they can reach is what is 'highly probable'. Human reason and testimony exclude divine faith. For instance, a man professes that he believes Jesus Christ to be the Son of God. Ask him why he believes this and he will say, 'Because God who cannot lie has revealed and declared him to be so.' Now ask him where or how God has revealed and declared him to be so, and he will answer, 'In the Scripture, which is his Word'. Now ask him why he believes Scripture to be God's Word, and if he does not have divine supernatural faith, he must answer, 'Because I have been persuaded by many good and strong arguments that it is highly probable that it is God's Word. These arguments have

[16]

persuaded me to believe Scripture to be God's Word, and I have every assurance that it is, for the men who gave me these arguments were good men, therefore I firmly believe Scripture to be God's Word.

But all these arguments are purely human and therefore fallible, and so it is possible they could be false. None of the arguments come from God's authority and truth. So this man's faith that Jesus Christ is the Son of God is both human and fallible and may be nothing more than a deceit and a lie. Human, fallible faith receives the Word of God as the word of man and not as it really is, the Word of God, contrary to the way in which the Christians at Thessalonica received it (*1 Thess.* 2:13).

If I believe Scripture to be the Word of God with a human faith only, I necessarily believe all that is in Scripture to be the Word of God by human faith only. But if I believe whatever is in Scripture with divine, supernatural faith, I must with the same faith believe Scripture itself to be God's Word. We must believe the revelation and the things revealed with the same kind of faith or we bring confusion into the whole business of believing. No man living can distinguish in his experience between that faith with which he believes Scripture and that with which he believes the doctrine of Scripture or the things in Scripture. Nor does Scripture teach any difference in the type of faith required. All our believing is based on the authority of God who reveals. The faith by which we believe Jesus Christ to be the Son of God is exactly the same faith by which we believe Scripture to be God's Word.

Some argue that Scripture truths have such a majesty, holiness and excellency about them and are so reasonable and so beneficial to those who are not prejudiced against them that they will of themselves convince any unprejudiced person who has a sense of his own need and who wishes to be blessed.

[17]

But I cannot completely agree with this for these two reasons, among others:

1. True faith is based on testimony. But the doctrines contained in the Scripture, or the subject-matter of the truth to be believed, do not themselves have the nature of testimony. The authority of God, and so his veracity, manifest themselves primarily in the revelation itself, before they do in the particular things revealed.

2. The excellency of the doctrines revealed in Scripture respects, not so much their abstract truth as their goodness and suitableness to the souls of men in their present condition. No one can have a due apprehension of that goodness unless his mind already assents to the things revealed, which is believing. So this cannot be the reason why we believe.

On this supposition the whole work of believing would be a work of reason. And this would then exclude the work of the Holy Spirit, which no Christian could agree to. Some doctrines revealed in the Scripture are far above human reason, such as the Trinity, the mystery of the one essence in three distinct Persons, the incarnation of the Son of God, the resurrection of the dead and many others. Flesh and blood does not reveal these things to our minds, but our Father who is in heaven.

Human reason without divine grace is not only weak and limited but also depraved and corrupted. The fleshly mind cannot subject itself to the authority of God in any supernatural revelation whatever. So the unrenewed man cannot receive it as from God but rather sees it as 'foolishness' and most undesirable.

Therefore we need to turn to the Holy Spirit to believe Scripture to be the Word of God. It is his work to create in us that divine supernatural faith without which we cannot believe anything that is divine and supernatural.

[18]

Doctrine: The divine, supernatural faith by which we believe Scripture to be the Word of God is wrought in us by the Holy Spirit. Until this work is done in us, whatever arguments or reasons are put to us, we cannot believe Scripture to be the Word of God on the authority and truthfulness of God alone as we are required to do.

This work of the Holy Spirit can be denied only on two assumptions. The first assumption is that we are not required to believe Scripture to be the Word of God with a divine, supernatural faith, but only by human reason and testimony, and the second assumption is that this divine, supernatural faith is of ourselves and is not wrought in us by the Holy Spirit.

The first of these has already been disproved. The second assumption is ridiculous. If this faith is divine and supernatural it cannot be of ourselves, but must be of God. Those of the church of Rome who would have us subject our faith to the authority of their church, yet subjectively acknowledge the work of the Holy Spirit working faith in us, and that work they admit to be necessary to our believing Scripture rightly. They assert that without supernatural assistance there is in no man any true faith at all. Neither the light of the sun, nor any persuasive arguments given to men to look up and see the sun, will enable them to discern it unless they have eyes to see it.

This truth is not denied by any in express terms that I know of. All that which is properly called faith, that which truly believes divine revelation to be divine revelation on the authority and truth of God, that faith which is acceptable with God, is the work of the Spirit of God in us. And this cannot be questioned by any who believe the gospel.

The Holy Spirit enables the soul to come to a divine supernatural faith by *illuminating the mind*. The effect of this work of illumination is a supernatural light by which the mind is renewed

(*Rom.* 12:2; *Eph.* 1:18–19; 3:16–9; *Deut.* 29:4; *1 John* 5:20; *1 Cor.* 2:14; *John* 6:45; *2 Cor.* 4:6). By this renewing of the mind we are enabled to discern the evidences of the divine origin and authority of Scripture that are in Scripture itself as well as to assent to the truth contained in Scripture.

Without this renewing of the mind we cannot do so, for the 'natural man does not receive the things of the Spirit of God for they are foolishness to him, neither can he know them for they are spiritually discerned'.

That there is a divine and heavenly excellency in Scripture cannot be denied, for all the works of God set forth his praise. It is impossible that anything should come directly from God without the stamp of divine excellencies upon it. But these excellencies we cannot see or discern, however glorious and majestic they are, without the effectual work of the Holy Spirit illuminating our minds.

'For it is the God who commanded light to shine out of darkness who has shone in our hearts to give the light of the knowledge of the glory of God in the face of Jesus Christ' (*2 Cor.* 4:6). The Holy Spirit irradiates the mind with a spiritual light by which it is enabled to discern the glory of spiritual things. Those whose minds have not been so illuminated cannot discern the glory of spiritual things because they are those 'whose minds the god of this age has blinded, who do not believe, lest the light of the gospel of the glory of Christ, who is the image of God, should shine on them' (*2 Cor.* 4:4). Those who are under the power of their natural darkness and blindness cannot see or discern that divine excellency in the Scripture and so cannot believe it aright to be the Word of God. They may assent to the truth of Scripture and that it is from God purely on human reason and argument, but cannot believe it to be God's Word with a divine, supernatural faith.

There are two things which prevent men from believing Scripture to be the Word of God with a divine, supernatural faith.

The first is *the natural blindness and darkness of their minds* which have come upon all men by the Fall and by the depravity of their natures, and the second is that through the craft of Satan, *their minds are held by prejudices* received from tradition, education and desires for worldly popularity and praise. Man needs to have this blindness and darkness of mind removed. So David prays that God would 'open his eyes that he might see wondrous things out of his law' (*Psa.* 119:18). He prayed, 'Make me understand the way of your precepts' (*Psa.* 119:27). He also prayed for 'understanding' so that he would be able to keep the law (v. 34). So the Lord Christ also 'opened the understanding' of his disciples so that they 'might comprehend the Scriptures' (*Luke* 24:45. See also *Matt.* 11:25; 13:11).

ILLUMINATION AND REVELATION

This illumination of the mind by which light is communicated to the mind, Scripture calls 'revealing' and 'revelation' (*Matt.* 11:25, 27). So Paul prays for the Christians at Ephesus that 'God would give them the Spirit of wisdom and revelation in the knowledge of Christ' (*Eph.* 1:17–19). It is true that these Christians at Ephesus were already believers or considered by Paul as such. But if he judged it necessary to pray for them that they might have 'the Spirit of wisdom and revelation to enlighten the eyes of their understanding', so that they might grow in faith and knowledge, then it is much more needed to lead unbelievers into that faith which is divine and supernatural, which, in their state of unbelief, they did not and could not have.

[21]

This illumination of the mind is not the discarding of all rational arguments to admit extraordinary direct revelations, such as were granted to the prophets, apostles and others whom God used to write the Scriptures. The revelation we mean differs completely from direct, external revelations.

Those direct, external revelations given to the prophets and apostles dealt with things not previously revealed (*Eph.* 3:5, 9–10). Direct, divine, prophetical revelation, lies in direct inspiration from God, or in visions and voices from heaven accompanied by the power of the Holy Spirit temporarily affecting the minds and guiding the tongues and hands of those to whom these revelations were granted, like musical instruments played with a skilful hand.

The revelation or illumination we mean is that work of the Spirit which frees our minds from darkness, ignorance and prejudice, enabling them to discern spiritual things rightly.

It is this work of illumination by the Spirit that we need to seek in prayer.

It only remains to enquire whether we believe Scripture to be God's Word by the *direct internal testimony of the Holy Spirit* assuring us that it comes to us with divine authority. Is this testimony of the Holy Spirit distinct from the work of spiritual illumination? It is the common opinion of Protestant divines that the testimony of the Holy Spirit is the basic reason why we believe Scripture to be the Word of God. What they mean by this we shall look into. But it is because of this teaching that Protestants are generally said by the church of Rome and others to base all their reason for and assurance of faith in subjective feelings and experiences, thus exposing themselves to endless delusions.

THE INTERNAL TESTIMONY OF THE SPIRIT

What then is meant by this *internal testimony of the Spirit*? An internal testimony of the Spirit may mean *an extraordinary inspiration or new direct revelation by which Christians are given special assurance that Scripture is God's Word,* such as the assurance that was given to the prophets and apostles who received direct revelations from God. This assurance is independent either of the authority of the church or of any human arguments or reasonings. But this is not what we mean here by the internal testimony of the Spirit. Our faith in Scripture as God's Word is not based on any such private testimony given by the Holy Spirit. Nor is it based on any subjective feelings or experiences, for the following reasons:

1. Since the completion of Scripture, the church needs no new extraordinary direct revelations from God. This would overthrow the perfection of Scripture.

2. Those who are to believe will not be able, if new revelations are still being given, to protect themselves from delusions and from being imposed on by the deceits of Satan. New revelations are either to be tried by Scripture or they are exempt from such trial. If tried by Scripture, then these new revelations acknowledge Scripture to be a superior rule, judgment and testimony. So these new revelations cannot be that on which our faith can ultimately rest.

But if exempt from such trial by Scripture, these new revelations must produce a certificate for such exemption, or they must declare what are the grounds and what are the evidences of their own 'self-credibility', and how they may be infallibly distinguished from all delusions, and this can never be done. No subjective testimony can be the basis of faith or be the reason why we believe.

[23]

3. In the providence of God, generally, all who have given themselves up to pretended new revelations, though they have pleaded that these new revelations are agreeable to Scripture, have been seduced into ideas and practices directly repugnant to Scripture itself.

Nor is the internal testimony of the Spirit a further work by which our hearts, by the power of the Spirit, assent to the truth without hesitation, with an assurance above all human judgment and reason, standing in need of no further arguments or testimonies. This cannot be the basis of our faith in Scripture for the following reasons:

1. This supposed internal testimony of the Spirit does not have the proper nature of a divine testimony. It may be a divine work, but it is not a divine testimony.

2. The reason why we believe must be the same for all believers. The question is not how we came to believe, but on what testimony did we believe and do we believe? The object held out for faith to take hold of must be the same for all. Therefore the reason why we believe must be the same for all. But the above supposition makes as many different reasons for believing as there are believers.

3. On the above supposition, it cannot be the duty of anyone to believe the Scripture to be the Word of God who has not received this internal testimony of the Spirit. Where the true reason for believing is not put to us, there is no duty to believe.

But that work of the Spirit which may be called *an internal real testimony* produces stability and assurance of faith through his working in us in two ways:

1. He gives to believers *a spiritual sense of the power and reality of the things believed*, by which their faith is greatly established (*Col.* 2:2; *1 Thess* 1:5).

2. He *helps and relieves us against temptations to unbelief* so that they do not win the victory over us and helps us to deal with all attacks on the truth of Scripture. Arguments against Scripture will prevail against those who have an outward profession of the truth of Scripture without an experience of its power. They will prevail against those who allow the power of lust to lead them to rebel against the authority of Scripture and against those who allow their faith to be ruined by the scandalous quarrels and disputations of those of the church of Rome and others who decry the authority and truth of Scripture.

But against all these objections and temptations the minds of true believers are kept secure by supplies of spiritual light, wisdom and grace from the Holy Spirit.

There are several other special gracious works of the Holy Spirit on the minds of believers, which belong also to this *internal real testimony* by which their faith is established. Such are his 'anointing' and 'sealing' of them, his 'witnessing with them', and his being an 'earnest' in them. These will be dealt with later. By these works of his, our faith is increased and established daily more and more.

So, although no internal work of the Spirit can be the reason why we believe Scripture to be God's Word, yet it is such that without it we can never sincerely believe as we ought to believe, nor will our faith be established against temptations and objections of unbelievers.

5: Divine Revelation Itself the Only Foundation and Reason for Faith

What we have now prepared a way for is a direct answer to the question, *Why do we believe the Scripture to be the Word of God?* What is it that our faith rests on in this? What makes it the duty of every man to believe it to be so?

I answer, *We believe Scripture to be God's Word with divine faith for its own sake only.* The authority and truthfulness of God infallibly manifest themselves to our faith, or to our minds in the exercise of faith, by the revelation itself in Scripture, and not otherwise.

We do not believe Scripture to be God's Word on rational or scientific principles, because divine revelation cannot be proved by such means (*1 Cor.* 2:9). Nor do we believe it to be God's Word by human reasoning which only leads to high probability. Nor do we believe it to be God's Word because on moral grounds it is highly likely that it is. Many other things can be believed for these reasons which cannot be clearly proved (*1 Thess.* 2:13).

Scripture being God's Word proves itself so to be to my mind, soul and conscience by the revelation itself and in no other way. Scripture itself has its own power and ability to assure us of its divine authority.

Here we rest. If we do not rest our faith on this truth, we must run on the rock of a moral certainty only, which shakes the foundation of all divine faith. Or we must fall into the gulf and labyrinth of an endless circle, in proving two things mutually by one another, namely, proving the church by Scripture and Scripture by the church. Unless we intend to wander in such paths, we must come to something on which we may rest our faith for its own sake, and that not with a strong and firm opinion but with divine faith. And nothing can pretend to have such a privilege but the truth of God revealed in Scripture. Those who would have us believe Scripture to be the Word of God on the authority of the church telling us it is God's Word, though it may seem a ready and easy way to help our faith, yet when things come to be sifted and tried, we find all sorts of confusion in their arguments so that faith does not know where to stand or where to find rest.

Arguments to support the truth of Scripture's claim to be God's Word, all have their use in their proper place. These arguments are particularly useful when Scripture is attacked by atheism arising from the love and practice of those lusts and sins which Scripture condemns. With others, these arguments may help them to come to faith or might be the means of strengthening faith in those who already believe. But in my own experience, their use is not very great, nor have they ever been in the church of God. Most people who believe Scripture to be God's Word, do so without any help from these arguments, for many have not the ability to understand them.

The authority of the church witnessing to Scripture as God's Word is also helpful, but we do not believe Scripture to be God's Word because the church says so, but because Scripture says so. Yet the ministry of the church, as it is the pillar and ground of truth, holding it up and preaching it, is the usual way that men come to faith, for 'faith comes by hearing, and hearing by the Word of God'. We believe Scripture to be the Word of God for itself alone, but not by itself alone.

The ministry of the Word is the means which God has appointed for the declaration that the Scripture comes from God. And this is the usual way by which men come to believe Scripture to be God's Word. The church, through its ministry, witnesses to and avows Scripture to be God's Word. From

[27]

Scripture it teaches all sorts of persons and these, so taught, become aware of the truth and the power of the things taught. Thus Scripture gives birth to faith in itself as the Word of God.

Along with Scripture, witnessing to itself, there is the internal effectual work of the Holy Spirit begetting faith in us, without which we can believe neither the Scriptures nor anything else with divine faith, not for lack of evidences in them, but from lack of faith in ourselves.

So we declare that God requires us to believe Scripture for no other reason but because it is his Word. Scripture is God's revelation to us and we believe it on his authority and because he is truthful. The basis of our faith is, 'Thus says the Lord'.

REVELATION THE FOUNDATION OF FAITH

We will refer to some Scripture testimonies to show this:

1. *Deuteronomy 31:11–13*. Here God requires faith in and obedience to his law. He gives no proof that it is his law but the law itself. Those to whom it first came had miracles along with the giving of the law, but it is now to be taught to children of future generations who knew nothing of this. See also Deuteronomy 29:29, where 'revealed things' are said to 'belong to us and to our children for ever, that we may do all the words of the law', that is, that we might receive them as divinely revealed.

2. *Isaiah 8:19–20*. Here the question is, 'How can we be satisfied in our minds and consciences, or what is our faith and trust in?' Is it by direct diabolical revelations, either real or pretended, or by the written Word of God, 'the law and the testimony'. To the written Word we are sent. Those who go after supposed revelations prove that they have no light in them. But how shall we know that the law and the testimony,

this written Word, is the Word of God? And how shall we distinguish it from every other pretended revelation? This is shown in:

3. *Jeremiah 23:28–29*. Two persons claim to have divine revelations. There is the prophet who has a dream, a false revelation claiming to be from God, and there is the prophet who has God's Word. The difference between them is as clear as that between wheat and chaff. This is known by their different natures and effects. Pretended revelations are like chaff which every wind will scatter. The true Word of God is like a fire and a hammer. It is accompanied with such light and power that it soon reveals itself to the consciences of men as the true Word of God. So God calls us to rest our faith on his Word alone and to reject all pretended revelations.

But does this authority and power reside in Scripture itself? This is seen in:

4. *Luke 16.27–31*. The rich man in hell asks, 'Give men a mighty miracle and they will believe.' But Abraham points to the Word of God. 'If they will not believe God's Word', he says, 'a miracle will not persuade them.' What more mighty argument to persuade men of the immortality of their souls could there be than seeing one rise from the dead? This is what the man in hell thought. But he who was in heaven did not agree. The man in hell thought Scripture was not sufficient evidence. The man in heaven taught that Scripture had quite sufficient evidence and power to persuade men of its truth. So if men did not believe the Scripture to be from God, neither would they believe the miracle to be from God.

5. *John 20:30–31*. John in his Gospel confirms this truth. The signs Christ did prove him to be the Son of God. But how do we come to know and believe these signs?

John points us to that which is written by divine inspiration: 'These things are written that you might believe.' So the writings have in themselves sufficient evidence to prove they are of God. It is as if John said, 'The writing of these things by divine inspiration is sufficient to beget and assure faith in you, so that you may have eternal life through Jesus Christ.' This is similarly determined by the apostle Peter:

6. *2 Peter 1:16–21.* The question here is about the powerful coming of Jesus Christ. Was it to be believed, and if so on what grounds? Is this a cunningly devised fable, or an invention of madmen (*Acts* 26:24)? The apostles saw his glory and were eyewitnesses of his majesty. But how are we to believe? We have 'a more sure word of prophecy', the written Word of God which is the prophetic Word made more sure, and this is sufficient in itself to bring us to believe with assurance that what is written is of God. Might it not be another cunningly devised fable? 'No', says Peter, 'The writers of Scripture were moved and acted on by the Holy Spirit. So what was written carries its own divine proofs.' Plainly, that which Peter teaches us is, that we believe all other divine truths because Scripture teaches them, but we believe Scripture itself to be God's Word because it claims to be God's Word, or because 'holy men of God' wrote it 'as they were moved by the Holy Spirit.' So also in:

7. *2 Peter 3:2.* Our faith rests on the authority of God in the writings of the apostles and prophets, and so we are said to be 'built on the foundation of the apostles and prophets' (*Eph.* 2:20) There is also Paul's testimony:

8. *Romans 16:25–26.* That which is to be believed is the mystery of the gospel, kept secret since the world began, or from the giving of the first promise. It was not completely hidden

from men, but not fully revealed as it is now. This gospel God commands all men to believe and obey. But what reason are we given as to why we should believe it? This alone is proposed, namely the divine revelation through the preaching of the apostles and the writings of the prophets, for faith comes by hearing, and hearing by the Word of God (*Rom.* 10:17). This was Christ's way of begetting and confirming faith in his disciples (*Luke* 24:25–27).

From these and many other testimonies it is clear that it is Scripture itself, the Word or will of God as revealed or written which is to be believed and obeyed. We are to receive and believe Scripture to be God's written Word with divine and supernatural faith. No other reason or motive is given to us to encourage us to believe Scripture is God's Word, nor is any argument given us to assure us that we are not mistaken, but only Scripture's own claim to be from God and therefore to come to us with divine authority. This claim of Scripture makes it our duty to believe and obey, and at the same time makes our faith infallible and therefore a sure, stable, established faith.

The same reason which the apostles and prophets gave why men should believe Scripture to be the Word of God is also given to us (*1 Thess.* 2:13; *2 Pet.* 1:21; *Isa.* 8:20; *Mal.* 4:4; *Psa.* 19:7–9, 119). Their faith was in 'Thus says the Lord, the God of truth' (*John* 1:45; *Luke* 16:29, 31; *Matt.* 21:42, *Acts* 18:24, 25, 28; 24.14; 26:22; *Rom.* 3:2; *Gal.* 1:1, 8; *Acts* 28:23).

Scripture was always held out, as was all divine revelation, to be believed without any other proofs or evidences except its own authority and truth. No other evidences to support Scripture's claims were given by either Isaiah or Jeremiah. If other supportive evidences were essential, then those who disbelieved were guiltless because they were deprived of these other 'essential' evidences before they could believe.

[31]

But in whatever way Scripture was brought to people, especially by preaching, it was to be received and believed for its own authority and truth and not that of the preacher, even if accompanied by miracles (*Rom.* 16.25–26; 10:14–15).

If in order to believe Scripture to be the Word of God, we need more than ordinary preaching, and if that 'more' is not given, then men are guiltless who do not believe. But this 'more' is never given, nor is it ever needed, because Scripture carries its own evidences of being a divine revelation, and so men are guilty if they do not believe Scripture to be God's Word.

So it is clear that our faith is built on and resolved into *the Scripture itself,* which carries with it its own evidence of being a divine revelation. And therefore our faith ultimately rests on *the truth and authority of God alone,* and not on any human testimony, such as that of the church, nor on rational arguments or fallible human motives.

6: The Self-Evidencing Power of Scripture

It may be asked why, if Scripture proves itself to be the Word of God as the sun proves its existence by light and fire by heat, do not all who read Scripture admit that it is God's Word? What prevents some from seeing and believing this truth?

HOW WE ASSENT TO CLAIMS ABOUT TRUTH

We should consider, first, that there are three ways by which we accept a statement or claim to be true:

1. The first way is by inborn principles of natural light.
These correspond to instinct in irrational creatures. So God complains that his people neglected and sinned against the natural light which was in them, while brute creatures followed and obeyed their natural instincts (*Isa.* 1:3). Thus the mind embraces notions of moral good and evil, even when it does not comply with what these guide it to do (*Jude* 10).

2. The second way is by our reasoning ability.
By concluding one thing from another the mind is able to come to various degrees of certainty, depending on the nature and degree of the evidence it has. So it has a certain knowledge of some things, and in others it only has an opinion or persuasion, against the objections to the contrary.

3. The third way is by faith.
This is the power of our minds to assent to anything as true with no support from natural light or reasoning. It is our assent on *testimony*, which also has various degrees and is of various

kinds, according to whether the testimony it rests on is human or divine.

God makes himself known to us in three ways, corresponding to these distinct faculties of our souls:

1. *God makes himself known to us by the inborn principles of our nature.*

Man has an indelible sense of God's Being, authority and will. There are two things to be noted in this natural light. The first is that power of thought, understanding and assenting by which God reveals his Being and essential properties (*Rom.* 1:19). The second is that power of judging and concluding by which God makes known his sovereign authority over all to our consciences. By conscience we judge, and cannot help judging, ourselves and our actions in the light of the authority and judgment of God (*Rom.* 2:14–15).

2. *God makes himself known to us by our use of reason.*

He proposes his works of creation and providence to our consideration, to instruct us concerning his Being, nature and properties (*Psa.* 19:1–3, 8:3; *Rom.* 1:20, 21; *Acts* 14:15–17; 17:24–28, 29; *Isa.* 46:5–8; 44:18–20).

3. *God makes himself known to our faith.*

Faith is that power of our souls by which we are able to assent to the truth put to us upon testimony. God makes himself known to our faith by his Word, the Scriptures, as already shown. Here the appeal is not to our natural light or to our reasoning powers (*Rom.* 1–17; *Heb.* 11:1). 'Thus says the Lord', is the only ground and reason for our assent, which depends on testimony alone.

Natural light, reason and faith agree with one another. Any conclusion about the nature, Being or will of God that is directly contradictory to natural light and that which is presented to faith by divine revelation is not to be received as a divine revelation. This is the charge Paul makes against the heathen philosophers, that they became vain and foolish, for their reason began to draw conclusions directly contrary to the first principles of natural light and the unavoidable ideas they had within them of the eternal Being of God. And many of these philosophers have foolishly concluded that all things began by chance or are ruled by fate. This is directly contrary to the first principles of natural light, and so is not the effect of reason but mere delusion.

On this ground the Roman Catholic doctrine of transubstantiation is rightly rejected. This plainly contradicts both the physical senses and reason, both of which say that the bread is still bread and the wine still wine. But a supposed faith contradicts both the physical senses and reason by saying that the bread and wine have been literally and physically changed into the body and blood of Christ. Such a contradiction would make the ways by which God reveals himself contradict and interfere with one another, leaving us with no certainty in anything, divine or human.

Things are revealed to faith which are above natural light and reason, yet they are agreeable to enlightened reason and to a renewed nature. So also there are many things which reason can see which cannot be seen by the first principles of natural light. These three means by which God reveals himself to us must harmonize and agree with one another, but truths are not equally seen by all three. Natural light is subordinate to reason and both natural light and reason are subordinate to faith. Faith fixes its eyes on revealed truth. Reason follows faith's lead, and so long as reason fixes its eyes on faith, natural light will grow stronger. Natural light is taught by both faith and reason, and reason is taught by faith.

THE REVELATION OF GOD TO NATURE, REASON AND FAITH

The revelation which God makes of himself through natural light infallibly proves itself to be from him. Our assent to it is also infallible. Notwithstanding what a few atheistic sceptics have said, the light of the knowledge of God through the in-born principles of our minds and consciences is manifestly from him and infallibly certain, according to the capacity of our natures.

The revelation which God makes of himself to our reason by his works of creation and providence also infallibly evidences itself to be from him, so that it is impossible that we should be deceived in it, for, 'his invisible attributes are clearly seen, being understood by the things that are made, even his eternal power and Godhead, so that they are without excuse' (*Rom.* 1:20).

When men do not come to the right conclusion from the facts of creation and providence the fault is not in God's revelation of himself but in men's depraved, vicious habits of mind, their enmity against God and their dislike of him (*Rom.* 1:28; *Isa.* 46:8; 44:19, 20).

To our faith, God reveals himself by his Word, the Scripture, which he has magnified above all his name (*Psa.* 138:2), that is, he has implanted in it more about himself than he has in any other way by which he makes himself known to us. This revelation is not suited to evidence itself to the light of nature or to our reason, even though there are external evidences which make a great impression on reason; but it addresses that power of our souls which can give an assent to the truth on the testimony of the proposer, without any other evidence.

There is an instinct in brute creatures that resembles our inborn natural principles. They may so develop their instincts by

[36]

experience that it may seem as if they had the ability to reason. But what animals do not have is the power or faculty of assenting to things on testimony or witness. If our souls lacked this one ability of assenting to truth on testimony, all that would be left to us would not be able to guide us efficiently through the affairs of this natural life. This ability to assent to truth upon testimony, being the highest and most noble faculty of our minds, is the faculty to which divine revelation is proposed.

THE FAITH WHICH GOD REQUIRES

In the case of divine revelation, for our assent to be according to the mind of God, our minds must be prepared and assisted by the Spirit of God.

If I say to a man that the sun is risen and shines on the earth, if he questions or denies it, and asks me to prove it, it is sufficient for me to say, 'It proves itself by its own light.' If he then says that this is no proof to him because he cannot see the light of the sun, then it is a satisfactory answer to say that he is blind. If he is not blind, it is useless to argue with him because he is contradicting the witness of his own eyes and leaves himself with no satisfactory rule by which he could ever be convinced about anything.

So if I tell a man that the 'heavens declare the glory of God, and the firmament shows his handiwork', or that the 'invisible things of God from the creation of the world are clearly seen, being understood by the things that are made', and he asks me how I can prove this, it is a sufficient answer to say that these things in and by themselves prove the existence of the infinitely wise and powerful Creator, and that he ought to be able to reason that out for himself. If he says that it does not appear to him that the universe was ever created but that it only came into being by chance, then it is sufficient to say that he is delirious and does not have the use of his reason, or that he is arguing in express contradiction to his own reason, as the heathen philosophers admitted.

And if I declare to anyone that the Scripture is the Word of God, a divine revelation, and that it proves and manifests itself to be so, and he replies that by the use of his sense and reason it does not appear to him to be God's Word, then it would be a sufficient reply to secure the authority of Scripture (though other means might be used to convince him), to say, 'All men have not faith', in the light of which alone we can see the marks of its divine origin impressed on it.

Since the Scripture is a divine revelation, and since it is our duty to believe it to be so, our faith must be suited to receive such evidence as God is pleased to give that Scripture is his Word. God has appointed faith to receive divine revelation, and he rewards those who have faith and judges and condemns all who do not (*2 Chron.* 20:20; *Isa.* 7:9; *Mark* 16:16).

Faith is able to give a firmer and more assured assent than any given by reason in the best of its conclusions. This is because the power of the mind to give assent to testimony, which is its most noble faculty, is elevated and strengthened by the divine, supernatural work of the Holy Spirit, as before described.

All this confirms our earlier conclusion, that it is the authority and truthfulness of God, revealed in and by the Scripture, which is the basis of our faith in, or supernatural assent to, the Scripture as the Word of God.

SCRIPTURE MANIFESTED TO BE THE WORD OF GOD

Faith is *an assent upon testimony*, and divine faith *an assent upon divine testimony*. The Spirit testifies *to* Scripture, *in* Scripture and *by* Scripture, and he does this in two ways:

1. The Holy Spirit has put into Scripture impressions of divinity. All the divine excellencies, or properties of the divine nature, revealed in Scripture prove that testimony of the Spirit on which our faith rests.

We learn the eternal power and deity of God from the works of creation by those marks, tokens and impressions of his divine power, wisdom and goodness that are upon them. They are clearly seen by the things that are made. We need no other arguments to prove that God made the world but the world itself (*Psa.* 104).

Now there are greater and more evident impressions of divine excellencies left on the written Word from the infinite wisdom of its Author than any that are in the other works of God.

So David, comparing the works and the Word of God as to their power to declare the glory of God, ascribes much to the works of creation, yet prefers the Word incomparably before them (*Psa.* 19:1–3, 7–9; 147:8–9, 19–20). And these impressions of divinity reveal the Word to our faith to be his more clearly than the marks in creation do his other works to be his to our reason.

God, as the immediate Author of Scripture, has left in the very Word itself evident tokens and impressions of his wisdom, foreknowledge, omniscience, power, goodness, holiness, truth and other divine infinite excellencies, giving sufficient evidence to the enlightened minds of believers.

2. The Spirit of God testifies to the divine origin and authority of Scripture by the power and authority exercised by it over the minds and consciences of men.

The apostle Paul expressly affirms these divine effects to be the reason and cause of faith (*1 Cor.* 14:24–25). The acknowledgement given by an unbeliever that God is in or among his people is a profession of faith in the Word administered by them. Such persons assent to Scripture's divine authority, not through the force of any external arguments produced and pleaded with that purpose in mind, nor upon the testimony of this or that church, nor by seeing miracles, not even by the miraculous gift of tongues (*1 Cor.* 14:23–24), but only through that divine power of which they have found and felt the experience in themselves. 'He is convinced by all, he is judged by all.' He cannot but acknowledge that a divine power accompanied the preaching of God's Word. 'The secrets of his heart are revealed.' This must be the effect of divine power, since God alone is the searcher of hearts (see *John* 4:29; *Heb.* 4:12)

By the power of the Word sinners are converted to God, born again, created anew and raised from death to life (*1 Pet.* 1:23; *James* 1:18). By the same Word, the new nature is kept and preserved to eternal life (*1 Pet.* 2:2; *James* 1:21; *Acts* 20:32. See also *Rom.* 1:16).

The following are some other powerful effects of Scripture, proving it to be from God:

Scripture has power *to bring conviction of sin*. This is the first step in the conversion of sinners. This work on those who did not expect it, who did not desire it, and who would avoid it if they could, proves Scripture to be of divine authority.

Conscience is the territory or dominion of God in man. God has so kept conscience to himself that no human power can possibly enter into it or control it in any way. But in this work of conviction of sin, the Word of God, the Scriptures, enter into the conscience of the sinner, take hold of it, bring home to it guilt or peace, and that by its own laws or rules of evidence. Where the Word of God brings guilt, nothing in the world can bring peace. Where the Word brings peace to the conscience, nothing can trouble it. When this work proceeds, conscience immediately recognizes a new standard, a new law, a new government, God's holy Word. Conscience would not subject itself to Scripture if it did not have infallible evidence that it was indeed God's true Word (*1 Cor.* 14:24– 25; *2 Cor.* 10:4–5; *Jer.* 23:29).

Scripture has power *to enlighten men's minds*. Scripture is as a 'light shining in a dark place' (*2 Pet.* 1:19; *2 Cor.* 4:4, 6). Without Scripture men's minds are all darkness (*Isa.* 60:2). Scripture alone can remove the darkness of error, superstition, ignorance and prejudice (*2 Cor.* 3:18; 4:4, 6).

Scripture has power *to bring a sense of awe into men's minds*. Though men may hate its laws, despise its promises, laugh at all its threatenings, and approve of nothing in Scripture, yet even God's enemies cannot shake off a disquiet from the sense of its divine authority (*Psa.* 45:5).

Scripture has power *to bring strength and comfort*. Scripture proves itself to be God's Word by its power to bring strong consolation in the deepest and most unrelievable distresses, enabling believers to rejoice with joy inexpressible and full of glory (*1 Pet.* 1:6–8).

And there is a further peculiar work of the Holy Spirit by which he effectually assures our minds that the Scriptures are the Word of God, and by which we are ultimately established in the faith that this is so. And I cannot but marvel and bewail the fact that any who desire to be thought Christians should ever deny this.

7: The Kind of Assurance Scripture Brings

Three observations concerning the assurance which Scripture gives that it is the Word of God arise from what has been said:

1. *The simplest and least educated believer assents to Scripture as the Word of God with the same assurance as, and often with greater assurance than, the wisest and best educated believer.* Why is this so? No assent of the mind can have more assurance than the evidence itself gives. Nor can any evidence of truth beget an assent to it in the mind without being taken hold of and understood. So the evidence that Scripture is the Word of God must be capable of being perceived, taken hold of and understood by the least educated true believer. Therefore it cannot lie in subtle, learned arguments which cannot be understood by the uneducated.

The marks of divine wisdom, goodness, holiness, grace and sovereign authority implanted in Scripture by the Holy Spirit are as clear to the most ignorant and uneducated believer as to the most intelligent. And the least educated believer is as able to experience the divine power of Scripture as is the most learned. It must therefore be granted that the evidence through which Christians come to believe Scripture to be God's Word is equally obvious to all sorts of believers.

2. *The assent we give to Scripture as the Word of God is accompanied with more assurance than assent based on the best scientific demonstration.* The evidence given by science and human arguments affects the mind only. The evidence which we have by faith works effectually on the will also,

because of the goodness and excellence of the things believed. And so the whole soul adheres more firmly to the objects of faith than it does to things for which the evidence is clearer but in which the will and affections are little concerned.

The best, holiest and wisest men have cheerfully and joyfully sacrificed all their temporal interests and risked all their eternal interests on account of the certainty they had by faith that the Scripture is a divine revelation. Three things contribute to this certainty:

i. The ability to assent to truth upon testimony is the highest and most noble power or faculty of our rational souls. So when it has the highest evidence which it is capable of receiving, which it has in the testimony of God, then it gives us the highest certainty and assurance we can reach in this world.

ii. To come to this divine faith, a special internal work of the Holy Spirit is required. This makes it more than a natural act of our minds. So divine faith is higher and more excellent than mere scientific assent.

iii. The revelation which God makes of himself, his mind and will, by his Word, is more excellent and accompanied with greater evidence of his infinitely glorious properties than any other discovery of truth. In this alone the mind finds absolute rest and satisfaction and so has the highest assurance attainable in this life.

3. *Both the internal work of the Holy Spirit on the minds of men enabling them to believe and his external work giving evidence in and by the Scripture of its own divine origin are necessary to believing.* Those who would deny either are seeking to expel all true divine faith out of the world and to substitute in its place a mere probable persuasion.

OBJECTIONS

1. *If we take away the rational grounds on which we believe the doctrine of Christ to be true and divine, and leave only evidence which can be discerned by those who believe, how can we begin to convince unbelievers?*

Answer: Unbelievers are convinced by the power of the Spirit through the preaching of God's Word (*1 Cor.* 2:4–5; 14:24–25). Rational arguments can be used provided they are forcible, compelling, convincing and not open to doubt, and provided they are clearly shown not to be the sole basis and reason for believing. To plead the self-evidencing power of Scripture is not to deny the need for other arguments to silence atheists and further establish believers.

Normally God brings us to faith by the ministry of his Word. At first this was done by the *extraordinary* ministry of the apostles and prophets, and later by the *ordinary* ministry of pastors and teachers (*2 Tim.* 3:14–17). To those utterly unacquainted with the mysteries of the Word they preached the doctrines of Scripture, basing their preaching on the divine revelation given there. And this preaching of the gospel was not left by God to work itself into the minds of men by its own suitability, but God accompanied their preaching with divine power, making his Word effectual for their salvation (*Rom.* 1:16). Some derided and scorned this new doctrine. Others, whose hearts God opened to attend to it, embraced and submitted to it. After the propagation of the gospel, those born within the pale of the church were instructed both by the ministry of the Word and by other teachers.

In both cases those addressed are directed to the Scripture as the sacred repository of the revelation of God. Now as they begin to read the Scripture for themselves, God confirms this truth to their minds by his Spirit by impressing upon them the marks of divine wisdom and holiness implanted in Scripture, which they are now able to see and discern, and on which they now rest as the immediate Word of God. This was the case of the woman of Samaria and the inhabitants of Sychar with respect to their faith in Christ (*John* 4:42). This is the way by which men are usually brought to believe the Word of God (*Rom.* 10:14–15,17); not by external arguments or motives, by which no-one was ever converted to God, nor by simply handing them the Bible to read for themselves, nor by miracles, nor by immediate revelation or private subjective testimony of the Spirit. Nor is their faith a persuasion of the mind for which they can give no reason except that they are so persuaded.

2. *Either the evidence that Scripture is the Word of God is so clear that everyone must assent to it, or the evidence must lie in the working of the Holy Spirit in the minds of those to whom it is proposed.*

Answer: Firstly, all divines, ancient or modern, popish or Protestant, agree that a work of the Holy Spirit is necessary to bring men to believe Scripture to be God's Word. But they do not say that this work of the Holy Spirit is the *testimony* or *evidence* on which we believe Scripture to be the Word of God.

Secondly, we are not arguing about how the statement, 'Scripture is the Word of God', may be proved to mere reason, but how it is evidenced to our understanding, as able to assent to truth upon testimony.

It is by faith that we are obliged to receive the truth of this statement, infallibly, because the evidences and the testimony are infallible. The evidence and certainty involved are of a higher nature and of a nobler kind than the strictest demonstration in natural things or the most forcible argument in moral things.

3. *If this is true, then no-one can be obliged to receive Scripture as the Word of God who does not have faith. And none have faith except those in whom it is wrought by the Spirit of God.*

Answer: Firstly, this objection is irrelevant because the work of the Spirit is pleaded as the *actual cause* of our believing, not as the *objective reason* why we believe.

Secondly, we must not be ashamed to attribute all that is spiritually good in us to the work of the Holy Spirit, but what we are saying is that it is his work in us which is the *actual cause* of our believing, rather than that his inward testimony is the *basis* on which we believe.

Thirdly, we are obliged by God's commands to do many things which we are now utterly unable to do without his grace. We *ought* to see the evidence and believe, even if we cannot, without the work of the Spirit.

Fourthly, men are obliged to receive Scripture as God's Word on its own evidence so to be. Every true divine revelation has enough evidence accompanying it to *oblige* those to whom it comes to believe it, on pain of God's displeasure. God is not obliged to confirm every particular divine revelation with a miracle; and when he requires faith and obedience, men sin if they do not comply with his will.

Fifthly, even if this objection could only be answered by reducing the faith which God requires to a mere natural assent based on rational arguments, without any help from the Spirit, as some would argue, I would still ten thousand times rather accept all the real consequences of the objection than admit such a destruction of true divine faith as this would amount to. However, the idea that anyone to whom the Scripture comes is exempted from the obligation to believe because he lacks the aid of the Spirit is not one of those consequences.

4. *If true divine revelation is so clear, why are certain books of the Scripture received as canonical and others rejected?*

Answer: As to the books of the Old Testament, we have the canon of them given us in the New Testament where it is affirmed that to the church of the Jews were committed the oracles of God (*Rom.* 3:2). This both confirms all that we receive as canonical and excludes all that we exclude. And concerning the New Testament books, there are no claimants, nor were there ever any, that present any difficulties to anyone's faith.

All books that have claimed to be from God, or have been put forward by deceivers as being from God, have sufficient evidence in themselves of their human origin.

We need not refuse the ministry of the church, nor the help of providence, by which the Scripture has been brought to us, nor the light which one part of Scripture throws on another part. The Scripture is to be believed *for* itself, but not necessarily *by* itself, with no help from other means.

In all true books of Scripture, divine characteristics and criteria are present sufficient to distinguish them from all other books whatever and to testify their divine origin to the minds and consciences of believers. With all divine revelations, including the words of our Lord Jesus Christ, a sense of the power and efficacy of the truth proposed is required if they are to be believed (see *John* 8:30). Without this, even miracles will be despised, as they were by some who were afterwards converted by the preaching of the Word (*Acts* 2:13), or else they will produce only a false or temporary faith (*Acts* 3:7–10; 8:13, 21).

Part Two

Understanding the Mind of God

1: How We Learn the Mind of God from Scripture

The two springs from which all streams of light and truth flow to us are our belief that the Scriptures are the Word of God and our understanding of the mind and will of God as revealed there. It is therefore vitally important to us that these springs are not stopped up or polluted. If the pleasant streams running through our land are controlled by others who can intercept or poison them, we will always be dependent on those others for the benefit of them.

The Church of Rome has always sought to keep these two springs under her control. She says, firstly, that Scripture can only rightly be believed to be the Word of God on her testimony that it is; and secondly, she does not allow the people to interpret Scripture for themselves. They must interpret it according to the mind of the church. It is Rome that tells people what the Bible is and what it means and says. In Part 1 of this discourse, I have taken the first spring out of her hands. What now lies before us is to secure the right of all believers to the other spring also – *a right understanding of the mind and will of God as revealed in the Scriptures.*

My principal point is this: *Every Christian may, if he uses the means given by God, arrive with certainty at the truth revealed in Scripture. This understanding will be sufficient to guide the believer in the life of God, to deliver him from the dangers of ignorance, darkness and error, and to lead him to true blessedness.*

We have no need to depend on the 'authoritative interpretation' of any church or person whatever, though ordinary believers are obliged to make diligent and conscientious use of the ministry of the church as a means appointed by God to lead, guide and instruct them in the knowledge of God's mind and will revealed in Scripture.

If any man does not have full assurance of understanding of Scripture from God himself, but is dependent on the authority of men, he will never be able to suffer for the truth or perform any duty to God in a right way. Every believer must be able to say, 'I believe because of God's Word', not 'I believe because some church or man told me.'

The question then is: *How may anyone attain a right understanding of the meaning of Scripture, as God would have us know or believe it?* And the position I will seek to establish is this: *There is a special work of God's Spirit on the minds of men, imparting spiritual wisdom, light and understanding to them. This work of the Holy Spirit is essential to the understanding of the mind of God in his Word, and the understanding of the mysteries of heavenly truth contained there.*

THE WORK OF THE SPIRIT IS ESSENTIAL

No man can understand Scripture aright without the effectual help and assistance of the Holy Spirit. However, we reject all fanaticism and claimed prophetical inspirations. The Holy Spirit works through our reason, enlightening it and guiding it to right scriptural and spiritual conclusions. We do not need any new divine inspirations or revelations to enable us to interpret Scripture aright. The prophets and the writers of Scripture did not learn the mind of God in the revelation made to them, and by them to the church, solely through divine inspiration. These direct revelations and inspirations made to them were instead of the written Word. After they had received these divine revelations, they had to inquire into the mind and will of God in them in the same way as we do. As we have to study the Word of God written, they also had to study the revelations they were given (*1 Pet.* 1:10–11).

To understand Scripture rightly and arrive at the full assurance of understanding in the acknowledgement of the mystery of God we have no need to depend on the authority of any church whatever, though the true ministry of the church is of great use to all who need help.

However, we cannot arrive at a true understanding of Scripture merely by our own reason and insight, even if we use all the external means given to us to help us. For the right understanding of Scripture we are utterly dependent on the Holy Spirit. And there is a special work of the Holy Spirit in the supernatural illumination of our minds, enabling us to interpret Scripture aright. It is only by this work of the Spirit that we can arrive at that full assurance of understanding in the knowledge of the mystery of God. The Spirit's enlightening our minds, as we use our understanding, with the help of all external means, is the only safe way to arrive at a true understanding of God's mind and will in Scripture.

Therefore we conclude, *there is a special work of the Holy Spirit on our minds, enabling them to understand the Scriptures rightly.* But this special work of the Holy Spirit is quite different from all fanatical claims to inspirations and revelations, as we shall show.

2: Knowing the Mind of God: Some Teaching from Scripture Itself

T he whole of what was said in the previous chapter can be summed up in the prayer of the Psalmist, 'Open my eyes, that I may see wondrous things from your law' (*Psa.* 119:18). It is our duty to pray in the same way.

WHAT THE PSALMIST PRAYED FOR

He prayed that when he read the law his mind might be so illuminated that he would be enabled to see the wonderful things that were in it.

The word *law* (Torah) signifies 'instruction'. It is God's teaching or instructing us by the revelation of himself. The Old Testament is divided into three parts, the law, the psalms and the prophets (*Luke* 24:44). Here *law* signifies the five books of Moses. But as all Old Testament revelations were based on these five books and explained them, the whole of the Old Testament is usually called 'the law' (*Isa.* 8:20). What is intended therefore is the entire revelation of the will of God given to the church as the rule of its faith and obedience. So 'the law' is equivalent to Holy Scripture.

The Psalmist prayed to see the wonderful things that were in the law. The Hebrew word for 'wonderful things' is *niphlaoth*. It comes from the root *pala* which means 'wonderful', to be 'hidden', to be 'great' and 'high'. The word therefore refers to things which cannot be reached by human wisdom.

'Wondrous things' are those things that have such an impression of divine wisdom and power upon them that we rightly wonder at them. These things are far above the natural reason and understanding of men to find out and grasp. They are 'wondrous' or 'wonderful' because Christ, whose name is 'Wonderful' (*pala*), is in them (*Isa.* 9:6).

In Hosea God says, 'I have written for him the great things of my law, but they were considered a strange thing' (*Hos.* 8:12). They were 'great' or 'wonderful' things because they were above human reason, but the people neglected and despised them because they thought them strange and alien to them. And how many still despise and neglect the heavenly, spiritual mysteries of the gospel, thinking them strange!

'Wonderful things' in Scripture are those mysteries of divine truth, wisdom and grace that are revealed and contained there, especially as they relate to Jesus Christ.

The Psalmist's prayer teaches us three things about these 'wonderful things.'

1. They are recorded or laid up for us in Scripture and nowhere else. Scripture is the treasure chest of these 'wonderful things'.

2. It is our duty to discover them and to understand them.

3. Without divine help we are utterly unable to discover them. By his prayer, the Psalmist teaches us not to trust in our own wisdom, but to acknowledge that it is the special work of God by his Spirit to enable us to understand his mind and will as revealed in Scripture.

The Psalmist's prayer shows the work of God that is needed to enable us to discern and understand the wonderful effects of divine wisdom treasured up in Scripture. It is the 'opening of our eyes'.

There is a divine light in Scripture (*Psa.* 36:9; 43:3; 119:105). But there is also by nature a covering or veil on the eyes of the understanding of all men so that they are unable by themselves to see this divine light or anything else by it. This covering must be removed. The Psalmist prays, 'Reveal my eyes', by which he means, 'Take off the veil or covering from my eyes'. This 'veil' is our natural darkness, blindness and ignorance.

Someone may object: Paul tells us this covering is taken away in Christ, and that the Jews still have this covering over their eyes because they rejected Christ (*2 Cor.* 3:13– 14, 16– 18). Has not the answer to the Psalmist's prayer already come?

Answer: When Moses received the revelation of the law from God 'his face shone' (*Exod.* 34:29). Now in that revelation were wonderful things concerning Christ. He was in all that revelation, and was the purpose of it all. The whole ministry of Moses was but a testimony given to the things that were later to be spoken concerning Christ (*Heb.* 3:5).

This light did not shine immediately into the hearts and minds of the people. A double veil or covering hindered them from seeing Christ in the Mosaic revelation. There was the veil on Moses' face, and there was the veil on their own hearts. Moses covered his face with a veil because the people could not look at his face which shone so brightly. This illustrated the sombre truth that the people could not grasp the truth concerning Christ which was the substance and the whole purpose of the law.

The veil covering Moses' face symbolized the Old Testament wrapped up in types, shadows and dark parables. This veil was removed when the full revelation of Christ came in the gospel.

But there is another veil, a veil on the heart. This veil is taken away only in Christ, that is, it is only removed from those converted to God by the work of the Holy Spirit. The doctrine of Christ is no longer preached by means of Old Testament types and shadows but in the clear glass of the gospel. By the gospel the veil is removed from the face of Moses. But we still need the second veil of darkness and blindness to be taken away from our hearts by the Holy Spirit. This was prophesied by Isaiah who spoke of the 'covering covered', or double veil, on the face of all people (*Isa.* 25:7).

No doubt the Jews knew the literal sense of the Scriptures well. But they could not grasp the 'wonderful things' until Christ opened their understanding. And this he did with the two disciples on their way to Emmaus (*Luke* 24:44–45). They needed a direct, gracious work of divine power on their minds to enable them to see these 'wonderful things'. There would be no need of this gracious work of Christ if we could understand these things by our own reason and understanding. Distinct from the Scripture and Christ's preaching of it to the disciples we read, 'he opened their understanding'. By this can only be meant a real, inward work of grace enlightening their minds.

But there is also another place in Scripture which is highly relevant to our purpose. Paul prayed that God would, by his Spirit, enable the Christians at Ephesus to know and understand his mind and will revealed in Scripture (*Eph.* 1:17–19). And what he prayed for others we are to pray for ourselves. And God answers by enlightening the eyes of our understanding by a gracious work of the Holy Spirit.

WHAT PAUL PRAYED FOR

Paul prayed for a revelation, or a spirit of revelation, to be given to them. He does not pray for a direct, external revelation from God, for Scripture is the church's only rule of faith and obedience. He prays for an inward subjective revelation enabling our minds to understand things already revealed. This enabling of our minds to understand spiritual truths is the work of the Holy Spirit, the Spirit of revelation.

[55]

Paul prays that the Christians at Ephesus might be enabled to see the 'wonderful things' of God's glory, the hope of God's calling, the riches of his glory and the exceeding greatness of his power in those who believe.

These things are revealed in Scripture, but Paul prays that Christians might know them. The natural man cannot know them (*1 Cor.* 2:14). The Ephesians and all Christians were to pray to the God and Father of our Lord Jesus Christ for this knowledge. Paul renews his prayer later in the epistle (*Eph.* 3:14–19). By this prayer Paul teaches Christians that, after having used all rational and natural means and abilities to understand Scripture, they still needed their spiritual eyes opened and their minds enlightened. What arrogance then would it be for any to think they can understand the mysteries of the gospel without spiritual illumination, even supposing there was no depravity of mind, since these 'wonderful things' are divine.

Paul prayed that the 'eyes of our understanding may be enlightened'. The Psalmist prayed, 'Open my eyes'. This prayer for enlightenment implies a special work of the Holy Spirit, by whom the eyes of our understanding are enlightened.

The Person who will enlighten our understanding is the Holy Spirit. Paul prayed that God would give the Spirit of wisdom and revelation. The Holy Spirit is freely given by God the Father (*Eph.* 3:17; *Luke* 11:13). The ability to truly understand the Scripture is therefore a gift of God (*Matt.* 13:11). Whoever has this ability to understand the mysteries of the gospel has it by the free gift of God (*1 Cor.* 4:7).

Paul calls the Holy Spirit 'the Spirit of wisdom'. As such, he was given to Christ (*Isa.* 11:2–3). The Holy Spirit is wisdom in himself and he is also the giver of wisdom to all Christians. His work is to open our eyes, to illuminate our minds, to give us that wisdom which delivers us from being fools ourselves and from judging the 'wonderful things' of God to be foolishness. Wisdom is required for such a purpose as this (*Hos.* 14:9; *Dan.* 12:10). Not having this spiritual wisdom is the reason why wicked men take offence at and dislike the ways of God. They cannot spiritually understand them and so reject and despise them to their own destruction.

This wisdom is not in us by nature. Men are naturally 'wise in their own conceits,' which, if persisted in, becomes a hopeless frame of mind (*Prov.* 26:12). This often shows itself in pride of ability to understand spiritual things (*1 Cor.* 1:18, 23). Paul therefore shows us the way to true wisdom when he says, 'If anyone among you seems to be wise in this age, let him become a fool that he may become wise' (*1 Cor.* 3:18).

3: How Are Believers Guided into 'All Truth'?

Jesus said, 'When he, the Spirit of truth. has come, he will guide you into all truth' (*John* 16:13). The Holy Spirit is the Spirit of truth. He is truth essentially in himself, and he is the one who leads the church into all truth.

But what does Jesus mean by 'all truth'? He does not mean 'all truth' absolutely. The Holy Spirit's work is not to lead us into all historical, geographical, astronomical and mathematical truth. The Holy Spirit is to lead us into all truth concerning the mysteries of the kingdom of God, of the gospel, of the counsel of God about the salvation of the church by Christ (*Acts* 20:27). The Holy Spirit will lead us into all truth necessary for faith and obedience (*Acts* 20:21).

Each believer is led into all the truth necessary to his own state and condition, to enable him to do his duty and work (*Eph.* 4:7). Christ gives to each according to his measure and needs.

HOW THE SPIRIT LEADS INTO ALL TRUTH

The promises concerning the mission of the Holy Spirit in John's Gospel are not all to be confined to the apostles, nor to the first age or ages of the church (*John* 14:16–17, 20; *Matt.* 28:20).

Many things in these promises did apply particularly to the apostles and had their fulfilment on the day of Pentecost (*Acts* 2:1–4). The apostles were commanded by Christ to wait for the coming of the Holy Spirit before they engaged in their work (*Acts* 1:4). When fully empowered they were enabled to fulfil the tasks Christ called them to. But this promise (*John* 16:13) is not restricted to the apostolic office.

It is not an *external* guidance into all truth by the objective revelation of truth that is meant, for this kind of revelation is not granted to all believers, nor are believers to look for such revelations. And the revelation of truth by the preaching of the gospel is not what is meant, since this is common to all the world and not subject to any special promise.

So it is the *internal teaching of the Holy Spirit,* giving an understanding of the mind of God and of all revealed sacred truths, which is intended. It is the same as the promise, 'They shall all be taught of God' (*John* 6:45), for this is how we are taught of God, and in no other way. The Holy Spirit leads us into all truth by giving us that understanding of it which we ourselves are not able to arrive at (see *Acts* 8:31).

All spiritual, divine, supernatural truth is revealed in Scripture. To come to know and to rightly understand this truth in Scripture is the duty of all, according to the means which each enjoys and the duties which are required from them. To make this possible the Holy Spirit is promised to them.

Of ourselves, without his special assistance and guidance we cannot arrive at a true knowledge or a right understanding of the truth revealed in Scripture.

AN ANOINTING FROM THE HOLY ONE

There is also the teaching of 1 John 2:20, 27. By the *unction* and *anointing* which John mentions in this passage the Holy Spirit and his work is meant. That the Holy Spirit in his special work is called an *unction,* or is said to *anoint* us, is clear from many places in Scripture (see *Heb.* 1:9; *2 Cor.* 1:21–22). Spiritual unction is never ascribed to anything else in Scripture. The expression 'from the Holy One' refers to Jesus Christ and is the fulfilment of Christ's promise to send the Holy Spirit to us to teach us and to lead us into all truth (*Acts* 3:4; *Rev.* 3:7). So the Holy Spirit is called 'The Spirit of the Lord', or 'of Christ' (*2 Cor.* 3:17–18; *Rom.* 8:9; *Phil.* 1:19).

The Spirit's 'abiding in us' repeats the promise of Christ that he, the Holy Spirit, will 'abide with us for ever' (*John* 14:16). The work attributed to this 'unction' is the same work ascribed to the Holy Spirit (*John* 16:13). The essential *truth* of the Holy Spirit is also declared in verse 27, 'The same anointing . . . is *true*, and is not a lie.'

The first thing ascribed to this 'unction' is the effect of his work in believers. They 'know all things'. The 'all things' here mentioned are all things necessary to our being ingrafted into Christ and our abiding in Christ (*1 John* 2:24). Such are the fundamental, important truths of the gospel. Believers may be ignorant of the doctrine of some truths, and may have little knowledge of anything, yet they shall know the mind and will of God as revealed in Scripture, in order that they may believe to righteousness and make confession to salvation.

The special purpose of the unction then was to preserve and deliver from the antichrists and seducers of those days. In the same way we also are preserved and delivered by the assured knowledge of the truths of the gospel as they are revealed in Scripture.

Believers 'do not need that anyone should teach them'. This refers only to the essential truths of salvation, of being ingrafted in Christ and abiding in Christ. Also, it refers to these essential truths absolutely, rather than to degrees of knowledge of them. A major part of the work of the ministry is to bring on believers to perfection in the things in which they have already been substantially instructed. What is chiefly meant by this statement is that believers need not depend on the light and *authority* of the teachings of men. None can be lords of our faith. They can only be helpers of our joy.

THE NATURE OF THIS WORK OF THE SPIRIT

The Holy Spirit does this work by *teaching*. 'The unction teaches you.' This does not refer to his direct inspiration, that is, his bringing new sacred truths from God directly to the minds of men. This is how he taught the apostles and prophets (*1 Pet.* 1:11–12; *2 Pet.* 1:21). Nor does God grant new revelations to preserve his people from error. God has made sufficient provision in his Word for that (*Isa.* 8:20; *2 Pet.* 1:19).

The teaching referred to is his *enabling us to discern, know and understand the mind and will of God as revealed in the Scriptures.*

It is not enough simply to know the truth. We must also be assured in our minds that we do really know it (*Eph.* 4:14; *Col.* 2:2). This assurance is given by the Holy Spirit 'who is truth and is not a lie'. There is no possibility of anyone being deceived in what he is taught by this 'unction'. The Holy Spirit gives to believers a secret witness to what he teaches, along with his teachings (*1 John* 5:6). There is a special power accompanying the teaching of God by his Spirit (*Job* 36:22; *John* 6:45). So whoever is taught in this way certainly believes the things he is taught, having the evidence of the truth of them in himself (*1 John* 5:10).

Spiritual sense and judgment are able to discern the divine evidences in the things the Holy Spirit teaches (*Heb.* 5:14). This is what gives the mind the highest assurance of the truth that it is able to have in this world.

The testimonies we have considered are sufficient to establish this first general assertion: *It is the Holy Spirit who teaches us to understand aright the mind and will of God in the Scripture.*

Without his aid we could never do this usefully and profitably to our souls.

The great promise of the New Testament is that all believers shall be 'taught by God' (*John* 6:45; see also *1 Thess.* 4:9). No man is *self-taught* in sacred things.

Who will the Holy Spirit teach? He will teach those who are meek and humble, those who give themselves to continual prayer, meditation and study in God's Word day and night, and those who strive to conform their lives to the truths he instructs them in. Because these are hard conditions to flesh and blood, there are few who apply to study in the school of God, while many will apply to other teachers, especially to the church of Rome, where no cost in self-denial need be involved.

DIFFERENT KINDS OF KNOWLEDGE

Many seem to attain to great knowledge in Scripture without the inward illumination of the Spirit. However, there is a difference between the Greek 'gnosis', meaning *knowledge*, and 'epignosis', meaning *acknowledgement*. The former, on its own, affects only the speculative part of the mind. It does little good and much harm. It is the knowledge that puffs up (*1 Cor.* 8:1).

The latter knowledge, on the other hand, gives the mind an experience of the power and force of the truth, transforming the soul and all its desires, bringing the 'full assurance of understanding' to the mind itself (*Phil.* 1:9; *Luke* 1:4; *Col.* 1:6, 9, 10; 2:2; 3:10; *Rom.* 10:2; *Eph.* 1:17; 4:13; 1 Tim. 2:4; *2 Tim.* 2:25; 3:7; *Titus* 1:1; *2 Pet.* 1:2, 3, 8; 2:20). This knowledge is only attainable by the saving illumination of the Spirit of God.

Men may have a knowledge of words and the meaning of propositions in the Scripture without a knowledge of the things themselves (*2 Cor.* 3).

This knowledge only informs the mind but does not really illuminate and enlighten it. So theology has been turned into an art or science instead of a spiritual wisdom and understanding of divine mysteries (*Rom.* 12:2).

This knowledge does not bring to 'all riches of the full assurance of understanding, to the knowledge of the mystery of God' (*Col.* 2:2). Nor has it any purifying effect (*1 John* 3:3).

It does not enable men to trust in God and cling firmly to him by love (*Psa.* 9:10). To 'know the name of God' in this Psalm is to know the revelation that he has made of himself, his mind and his will in Scripture. This enables us to 'try the spirits'.

There are three errors to avoid. Some pretend to be guided by the Spirit and neglect the written Word. Some despise the teaching of the Spirit and trust to their own understanding of the Word. Others reject both the Spirit and the Word and go after another rule and guide.

To none of these is the promise of the Spirit given. They are left to their foolish, corrupt imaginations.

Scripture is the believer's rule and the Holy Spirit is his guide.

Do we continue in prayer, and abound in prayer, as we ought, for that Spirit who alone can lead us into all truth? For that unction which teaches us all things with assurance and experience? There is no duty in this world more acceptable to God than fervent prayers for a right understanding of his mind and will in his Word. On this, everything else depends.

4: How Does the Holy Spirit Enlighten Our Minds?

We have sufficiently established our first general assertion, that we need a special work of the Holy Spirit in the illumination of our minds if we are to understand the mind of God as revealed in Scripture.

But some object that *we need no other assistance from the Spirit for the right understanding of Scripture than his general blessing on our own endeavours.*

To answer this we must consider the description of this work of the Spirit given in Scripture, and its effects in our minds. Various expressions are used in Scripture to describe this work:

1. It is called *the opening of our eyes, the enlightening of the eyes of our understanding* (*Psa.*119:18; *Eph.* 1:18).

2. It is called *a translation out of darkness into light* (*1 Pet.* 2:9; *Col.* 1:13; *Eph.* 5:8).

3. It is called *giving us an understanding* (*1 John* 5:20; *John* 17:3; *1 Cor.* 1:23–24; 2:14).

What is this 'understanding'? In every other place where the Greek word occurs, the essential faculty of our souls called understanding is meant (*Matt.* 22:37; *Mark* 12:30; *Luke* 10:27; *Eph.* 1:18; 2:3; 4:18; *Col.* 1:21; *Heb.* 8:10; *1 Pet.* 1:13; *2 Pet.* 3:1). It seems to be distinguished from the 'mind', and to mean the mind in *actual exercise*. But the understanding given us is not the natural and essential faculty of our souls but *a power and ability of mind to receive and apprehend the divine revelation given in the gospel.*

And this ability is *given* to us (*1 John* 5:20), which implies that it is more than an outward presentation of truth. If all that is meant by 'giving us an understanding' is a mere outward preaching of spiritual truths, then any preacher can give us such an understanding. But many who heard Christ preach did not understand because of the corruption of their minds.

4. It is called *teaching, leading and guiding into the truth (John* 6:45; 16:13; *1 John* 2:20, 27), as we have already seen. Two things are presupposed by these expressions. Firstly, a mind capable of being taught, led and guided into all truth, and secondly, teaching suited to that ability.

Some say that this teaching consists of a direct infallible inspiration of the same nature as that of the prophets and apostles of old. This takes away the distinction between the extraordinary and the ordinary gifts of the Spirit. Then it would not be true that God set in the church 'some prophets' (*Eph.* 4:11), since all were to be prophets. It also demeans Scripture, reducing it to the level of these supposed inspirations. The claim to such direct revelations always leads to contradictions among those who pretend to them. This in turn leads to confusion, unbelief, and finally to atheism. The prophets themselves did not have the knowledge and understanding of the mind and will of God which we are speaking of merely by direct inspiration. They too had to search into these revelations, as we do into the written Word (*1 Pet.* 1:10–11). Hence they frequently and fervently prayed for understanding, as we have seen in the case of David.

Others say that the understanding which is given consists merely in the outward preaching of the Word and the ministry of the church. But it is more than this, since everyone who is given this understanding actually comes to Christ (*John* 6:45), which does not happen through mere outward instruction.

The true meaning of 'an understanding' being given is that it is an inward work of the Holy Spirit giving light, wisdom and understanding to our minds (*1 John* 2:20, 27). It is by an 'unction' that we are thus taught, as we have shown. This is a

[65]

real giving of supernatural gifts and graces, and supernatural light is specially necessary for this purpose. These things were given in all their fulness to Christ, and were *his* unction or anointing (*Heb.* 1:9; *Isa.* 61:1). So our partaking of them in our own measure is *our* unction or anointing.

This does not mean that we do not have to make use of our own efforts and abilities to understand Scripture, but that we need the inward, effectual work of the Spirit along with the outward means of teaching and learning. The Ethiopian eunuch could not understand the Scripture and needed a guide to help him. Philip opened up the Scripture to him, but it was the Spirit who opened his heart to understand it, as he did the heart of Lydia (*Acts* 16:14).

5. It is called *a shining into our hearts* (*2 Cor.* 4:6). The truth and doctrine concerning Christ's Person and mediation are so presented and taught in the gospel that the glory of God is wonderfully represented by them. In the gospel is revealed what we are to know of God, his mind and will. God is revealed and declared by and in Jesus Christ.

Why is it, then, that all do not see 'the glory of God in the face of Jesus Christ' when the gospel is preached?

The first reason is *the effect of the power, temptations and suggestions of Satan* (*2 Cor.* 4:4). But even apart from this, there must be *a divine light shining into our hearts* to enable us to see that glory. The preaching of the truth is the outward objective light. The enlightenment of the Spirit is the subjective, inward light wrought in us when he takes away our natural blindness of heart.

The *effect* of this work of the Holy Spirit on the minds of men shows of what nature it is. It also is variously described.

It is called *light* (*Eph.* 5:8). By the work of the Holy Spirit we are made 'light in the Lord'. Light in the mind is the spiritual ability to discern and know spiritual things as Paul declares (*2 Cor.* 4:6). This is a work of the Holy Spirit in us. He who is 'darkness' cannot make himself 'light in the Lord'.

It is called *understanding* (*Psa.* 119:34; *2 Tim.* 2:7; *Job* 32:8).

It is also called *wisdom* (*Col.* 1:9; *Dan.* 12:10; *Hos.* 14:9; *Psa.* 107:43).

We have therefore shown that *there is an effectual operation of the Spirit of God on the minds of men enabling them to perceive and understand the supernatural revelations given in Scripture,* and we have also declared *the nature of that work, and the effects of it on our minds.* And no-one can understand the mind and will of God as revealed in Scripture without this special aid and illumination of the Spirit of God.

[67]

5: Hindrances to the Understanding of the Mind of God in Scripture

God has revealed his mind and will concerning everything necessary for his worship, and our faith and our obedience in it, in Scripture, as we have shown.

Why then do so much ignorance and so many misapprehensions of the mind of God as revealed there exist? Why are professing Christians so divided among themselves as to the right form of worship and other Christian doctrines? Because of these divisions, scandals and animosities, sometimes even leading to violence, some have drifted into atheism and others into indifference to all religion.

A full enquiry into the reason for all this darkness and ignorance among those who outwardly acknowledge the same gospel would require much time and diligence to handle the subject properly. At present I will only point to a few things, the consideration of which may help us to understand the matter.

THE REASON GIVEN BY THE CHURCH OF ROME.

All these things happen, say those of the Roman church, because of the obscurity, difficulty and perplexity of Scripture. 'If men trust to Scripture as their only guide they are bound to go wrong', they say. 'Therefore, trust the church, which cannot err or deceive.'

This is like shifting the blame for our own sin and unbelief to Scripture, as Adam did when he charged his sin upon Eve: 'The woman whom you gave to be with me, she gave me the fruit of the tree, and I ate' (*Gen.* 3:12). But surely we should seek the cause of these evils, not in God and his revelation, but in ourselves. Has God made his revelation dark, obscure and puzzling? Shall we say with Adam, 'The Scripture you gave us deceives us'?

THE TRUE REASONS

No, the first and general cause of all ignorance, error and misunderstanding of the mind and will of God as revealed in Scripture, among all sorts of men, is *the natural vanity and darkness with which the minds of all men are corrupted and depraved.* The minds of all men are naturally prejudiced by this darkness and vanity, and cannot be delivered from it except by the saving illumination of the Spirit of God.

By this darkness the mind is kept from discerning the glory and beauty of spiritual, heavenly truth and from being aware of its power and force (*John* 1:5). By the same means man is inclined to everything that is vain, foolish, superstitious and fleshly. He enjoys those things which rouse his pride, lust and all manner of corrupt desires.

Let us then learn from these wranglings among professing Christians *the sad corruption and depravity of our minds in our state of apostasy from God.* Let us make use of these things:

1. *To impress a due sense of our own condition upon our minds, so that we may be humbled.* To be lifted up is to be in great danger of departing from God (*Hab.* 2:4, with *Heb.* 10:38). We are by nature children of wrath, as others are, and have every reason to be humble.

2. *To learn to pity those still ignorant of spiritual things.* The merciful High Priest of the whole church has 'compassion on those who are ignorant and going astray' (*Heb.* 5:2). We should be like him here if we desire to be like him in glory. We are to have compassion on some, and others to save with fear, pulling them out of the fire (*Jude* 22–23).

[69]

3. *To promote gratitude to God,* who alone has brought us out of darkness into his marvellous light.

The second general cause of ignorance and error is *the corrupt desires prevalent in the minds of men* which hinder the right understanding of the mind of God in Scripture. It is because of these corruptions that the mind twists and perverts the truth, or is filled with prejudice against it (*2 Pet.* 3:16; *1 Tim.* 6:5; *2 Tim.* 3:8; *Eph.* 2:3). This state must be put right before we can receive God's Word with meekness (*James* 1:21).

The following are some of the corruptions prevalent in the minds of men:

1. *Pride or self-confidence* in our own wisdom and ability of mind to understand all the duties we owe to God. We think that by our own ability we can understand the mind and will of God, not realizing that this pride keeps our souls under the bondage of darkness and ignorance, and so we are led into foolish and pernicious errors.

2. *The love of honour and praise among men.* This desire presents an insuperable obstacle against the admission of sacred light and truth (*John* 5:44; 12:43).

3. *Holding stubbornly to a corrupt tradition and to deep-rooted errors.* This also prevents men from coming to true spiritual wisdom and understanding.

4. *Spiritual laziness* is of the same nature and effect. This prevails where we are reluctant to make the effort to come to a right understanding of what Scripture is saying.

5. *A love of sin,* causing us to hate the truth which condemns that sin (*John* 3:19–20).

6. *Satanic temptations and suggestions* (*2 Cor.* 4:4) hinder men from discerning the mind of God as revealed in the Scriptures.

Only the Holy Spirit can remove these hindrances and obstacles from our minds. He alone brings to our minds the spiritual light which scatters the darkness preventing us from seeing and understanding the mind of God concerning our eternal salvation.

The Holy Spirit particularly frees and purges our minds from corrupt desires and prejudices which are inbred, assumed by us or imposed on us. Our duty is to lay aside all these evils and receive with meekness God's Word which is able to save our souls (*James* 1:21). We are to cleanse ourselves from these things (*2 Tim.* 2:21). But we are to realize that without the help of the Holy Spirit we cannot rid our minds of them (*1 Cor.* 6:11; *Titus* 3:3–5; *Rom.* 8:13; *Eph.* 4:20–24).

The Spirit implants in our minds spiritual habits and principles opposing those corrupt desires. These habits and principles resist, subdue and expel the evil attitudes which fight against and pervert the truth. The new habits and principles are used by the Spirit to make us humble, meek and teachable.

Some who have despised or neglected this way of the Spirit have looked to divine revelations to overcome their wrong attitudes of mind. Instead, they have received diabolical delusions.

God has shown once and for all who they are who are fit recipients of divine teachings. They are the meek, the humble, the godly, who fear God, reverence his Word, submit their souls and consciences to his authority and resolve to obey all he commands (*Matt.* 18:3; *Psa.* 25:9; 12:19; *Prov.* 28:5).

If we would receive a true understanding of God's mind and will, we must pray that the Holy Spirit will bring us to such an attitude of heart and mind.

6: The Nature of Scripture, and the Right Approach to It

The next thing to be established is this: *The Holy Spirit has so prepared and arranged Scripture as to make it a sufficient and absolutely perfect way of bringing home to our minds that saving knowledge of God and his will which we need to live to him and come to the enjoyment of him in his glory.*

But we must observe, firstly, that the Spirit has not arranged the truths of Scripture into a theological system, order or method, like our systems of divinity, creeds, and confessions of faith.

And God's wisdom is seen in the arrangement of Scripture as it is. How many have received divine light and comfort suited to their needs from those occasional occurrences of truth found in the Scripture which they never could have received from a systematic theology! Scripture, like a good counsellor (*Psa.* 119:24), advises suitably to our situation and circumstances. The power and effect of the truth on our minds is often related to its arrangement and positioning. The way the Spirit has arranged the Scripture is the best for our needs.

In the composition of Scripture, the Spirit also took into account the various states and conditions of the church (*Heb.* 1:1). It was given for all ages, from the beginning to the end of the world. A system of doctrines would not have answered the ends of divine wisdom in teaching the church in all ages.

The aim of Scripture is to beget in men's minds, faith, fear, obedience and reverence to God; to make men holy and righteous, against all their own weaknesses, temptations and inclinations to the contrary. To make men humble, holy and wise in spiritual things; to guide us aright in our duties; to help us overcome temptations; to comfort us in all our troubles; to make us love God and live to his glory in all circumstances and situations – these ends, not systematic instruction, are the main purpose of Scripture.

The wisdom of God in Scripture is seen in the way in which it furthers other divine purposes towards the church, such as God's purposes in the great ordinance of the ministry. The minister is to search the Scriptures and to teach the mind of God from them (*Eph.* 4:11–16; *2 Tim.* 3:14–17). The Spirit could have so arranged Scripture as to make it clear and plain to every individual person without the help of the ministry. But the counsel of his own will (*Eph.* 1:11) was otherwise.

He wished to glorify his own power in bringing about great results by vile, weak means (*1 Cor.* 3:7; *2 Cor.* 6:7).

He wished to magnify his Son Jesus Christ in the communication of spiritual gifts (*Acts* 2:33; *Eph.* 4:8, 11–12).

He wished to show that in the work of his grace he would not destroy or contradict the faculties of the nature which he had created in the beginning, but would work on and change them, as he does by the ministry of the Word (*2 Cor.* 5.18–20).

The way Scripture is arranged also favours the duty of all believers to exercise faith and obedience. Each has to seek that part of Scripture that gives light and guidance in his particular needs and circumstances (*Prov.* 2:3–5). God has thus made it necessary for us to read the whole of Scripture and not to neglect any part of it.

Continual searching into the whole of Scripture will be blessed to our good, according to the prayer of our Saviour, 'Sanctify them by Your truth. Your word is truth' (*John* 17:17).

We must observe, secondly, that the Holy Spirit has so arranged Scripture that the mind of God in all things which concern our faith and obedience is clearly revealed in it.

However, we are to remember that Scripture is not the word of men but the Word of the living God. It does not necessarily have the artificial kind of clarity that men try to give to their writings, but it does have such a plainness and clarity as befits the holy, wise God, whose words are to be received with reverence, and with submission of mind and conscience. The appearance of obscurity arises from two causes: the *prejudices and corrupt inclinations* of those who come to Scripture with no intention of obeying it, and the *pride and self-confidence* of those who come to it in the supposed strength of their natural abilities.

Also the clarity of which we speak depends on the assistance of the Spirit of God of which we have spoken. Without this, the clearest revelations will appear dark and obscure, not from lack of light in them, but from lack of light in us.

DIFFICULT PASSAGES IN SCRIPTURE

Despite this clarity in Scripture there are still passages which are either (1) *hard to understand (2 Pet.* 3:16) or (2) hard to explain (*Heb.* 5:11), or interpret.

1. There are things which, in their own nature, are deep, wonderful, mysterious and exceeding our natural understanding and reason, in providence (*Psa.* 139:5, 6, 14–16) and in heavenly truth (*John* 3:12). The doctrine of the Trinity; the single divine nature in three Persons; the incarnation of Christ; the eternal decrees of God; the resurrection of the dead; the manner of the operation of the Spirit of God in regeneration – these are examples of the latter.

But whatever is necessary for us to believe concerning these things is plainly and clearly revealed in Scripture. The revelation is made in such statements and expressions as are clear and obvious to our understanding, even though we may not be able to comprehend them.

Rationalists make this most irrational statement: 'What we cannot comprehend in things divine and infinite, we will not believe, even though they claim to be revealed.' This wild and foolish principle leads straight to atheism, since the being of God is absolutely incomprehensible.

The degree of knowledge which we can reach about these deep mysteries is altogether sufficient for the purpose of the revelation itself. Our finite minds cannot perfectly understand things which are infinite. But the degree of knowledge to which we can attain is sufficient to produce, cherish, increase and preserve in us faith, love and holy obedience to his will, and to bring us to the enjoyment of God.

2. There are in Scripture things hard to interpret, not from the nature of the things revealed but from the way they have been revealed. Examples of these are allegories, parables, mystical stories, allusions, unfulfilled prophecies and predictions, references to the customs, persons and places of the time, computations of times, genealogies, the significance of words seldom used or used only once in Scripture, and the names of birds and beasts unknown to us.

But what is important to know and understand is plainly declared in some other part of Scripture. No doctrinal truth requiring obedience is obscure. In the Old Testament there are many revelations in types and allegories whose reality was Christ. What remains obscure is for the exercise of our faith, diligence, humility and dependence on God in our study of it.

As to prophecies of future upheavals in the church and the world, as in the book of Revelation, these had to be given in obscure, symbolical expressions, according to the nature of prophecy. It would have brought confusion on the works of God in the world and turned men away from simple obedience if they had been given as plain historical statements.

Some things are intentionally obscure, so that evil, perverse and proud men may stumble and fall at them, or be further hardened in obstinacy and unbelief (*1 Cor.* 11:19; *Jude* 4; *2 Pet.* 3:16; *1 Pet.* 2:8).

The Holy Spirit has given us a rule by which to interpret Scripture, which, while we follow it sincerely, will prevent us from sinfully corrupting the Word of God, even if we do not find the proper meaning in every particular place. This rule is the *analogy*, or *proportion*, of faith (*Rom.* 12:6). No Scripture is to be interpreted so that it contradicts something plainly declared elsewhere in Scripture. If we adhere to this rule, we shall not miss the mind of the Holy Spirit.

As to those things which are specially difficult, such as genealogies and chronologies and the like, they may be safely omitted by those who are not able to handle them so as to edify themselves and others.

Thus far we have dealt with the work of the Spirit in *preparing our minds* to understand the Scriptures, and his work in *preparing the Scriptures* for our understanding of them. It remains to consider the work of the Spirit and the help he affords in the *actual application of our minds to the understanding and interpretation of the Word*, and the means we are to use in this.

7: Means to be Used to Understand the Mind of God in Scripture

There are two kinds of means to be used for the right understanding and interpretation of Scripture: that which is absolutely necessary, and those additional means which help us to make a profitable use of Scripture.

As to the former, it is *diligent reading of the Scripture, with a calm, clear-headed consideration of what we read*. The whole of Psalm 119 sets out this duty and the benefits to be obtained by it. The eunuch read and pondered the prophecy of Isaiah, though he could not by himself attain the understanding of it (*Acts* 8:30–31).

More general and cursory reading of the Word in families and in private is also of great benefit, but what I chiefly intend is reading (or what is equivalent to it, having another read to us) which is thoughtful and contemplative, with inquiry into and meditation on the meaning.

As to the latter kind of means, by which we make our reading profitable, these may be divided into *spiritual, educational* and *ecclesiastical*. The first will be discussed in this chapter and the others in the next two chapters.

SPIRITUAL MEANS

Firstly, we must read Scripture with *fervent and earnest prayer for the help of the Holy Spirit* to enlighten our minds and lead us into the knowledge of the truth. This is of two sorts: prayer for the knowledge of the truth in general, and prayer for particular occasions, or particular places of Scripture whose meaning we seek.

This can certainly be laid down as a sacred truth: *Whoever, in the diligent and close study of Scripture, seeks to know the mind of God so as to obey him, and who continues in fervent prayers in and by Jesus Christ for supplies of the Spirit of grace to lead him into the full understanding of the truth as it is in Jesus, shall be kept from pernicious errors and will reach such a degree of spiritual knowledge as shall be sufficient to guide and keep him in the life of God for the whole of his faith and obedience.*

The second thing needed is *readiness to receive impressions from divine truths,* so as to have our minds and hearts conformed to the doctrine made known (*Rom.* 6:17; *2 Cor.* 3:18).

The third is *practical obedience in the course of our walk before God* (*Tit.* 1:1; *John* 7:17). It is by obedience to God's Word that we come to the assurance that what we know and learn is indeed the truth.

The fourth is *a constant desire to grow and progress in the knowledge,* out of love for the truth and the experience of its excellence (*Hos.* 6:3; *Prov.* 2:3–5).

And the fifth is *the use of ordinances of spiritual worship* as a means of growing in grace and in the knowledge of our Lord and Saviour Jesus Christ (*2 Pet.* 3:18), and this is further considered in Part 3 of the present book.

8: Tools from Various Disciplines to Aid in Our Understanding of Scripture

Educational means to aid in the understanding of Scripture include tools from various disciplines. These are neither good nor bad in themselves. The only measure of their value is the use they are put to and, in their application to the interpretation of Scripture, they can either be used well or thoroughly misused.

1. The first educational means is *a knowledge of and skill in the original languages* in which the Scripture was written, Hebrew and Greek. The Scriptures in these languages are peculiarly sacred and have a privilege above all translations. The words of the Scripture, being immediately given from God, show divine wisdom in every smallest detail and are all under the especial care of God, according to the promise of our Saviour (*Matt.* 5:18). There is a peculiar emphasis and energy in the originals of Scripture which cannot be completely translated into other languages, and such things as this cannot be appreciated except by those who are skilled in the original languages. It is also true, however, that such knowledge and skill can be used to fuel a profane pride and curiosity in sacred things.

2. The second educational means to be used to help reach a right understanding of God's Word is *a knowledge of the history and geography of the world*. This is of particular help in the understanding and interpretation of prophecies and chronologies, though it also is open to abuse, such as when knowledge from profane sources is used to cast doubt on the truth of Scripture.

3. The third educational means to reach a right understanding of God's Word is *skill in the ways and methods of reasoning.* The ability to judge how one thing depends on another, how it is deduced from it, follows from it, or is proved by it is helpful, especially in the understanding of Paul's epistles. What is the purpose of the writer of a book or an epistle? How does he develop that purpose? How does he confirm and illustrate it? The art of reasoning is especially important to those who undertake a series of expositions of Scripture. Without this ability they may well find themselves entangled and at a loss as to how one discourse logically follows from another. But all our skill in the art of reasoning must be subject to the wisdom of the Holy Spirit in Scripture.

While these educational means may all be helpful, they are no substitute for the peculiar work of the Spirit of God in the illumination of our minds. However skilled we might be in these methods, without the illumination of the Spirit we would still not understand any of the mysteries contained in the Word of the living God.

9: Help from the Church to Understand Scripture

There are also means and helps for the understanding of Scripture supplied by the ministry of the church in all ages. Three have been proposed: *catholic or universal tradition, the unanimous consent of the Fathers,* and *the writings of godly men who have gone before us.* How useful are these proposed helps?

1. *Catholic or universal tradition*

Some say that Scripture is to be interpreted only according to catholic tradition. I would be glad to have an interpretation of the whole of Scripture or of any passage in Scripture based on that rule. The truth is that no such agreed tradition exists. Scripture itself is the only catholic and universal tradition that we have.

No-one today can prove his interpretation of any part of Scripture to be correct according to catholic or universal tradition other than by showing that his interpretation is agreeable to the rest of Scripture, unless we accept that the meaning given to Scripture by some men who call themselves 'the church' was infallibly the mind of Christ and his apostles and of all true believers since.

2. *The unanimous consent of the Fathers*

The second ecclesiastical help put forward is that Scripture should be interpreted according to the unanimous consent of the Fathers.

But no-one who has read or considered the Fathers with attention and judgment can seriously accept this rule. How can those who so disagree among themselves be an authentic rule to others? It is true that they agree more on articles of faith than on exposition of Scripture, though even here they express themselves differently. But in exposition they really disagree frequently, and it is exposition that concerns us at present. We grant the Fathers' piety and ability, but they are not a rule to us.

3. *Scriptural writings of godly men*

This is the only ecclesiastical means that will help in the interpretation of Scripture: the light, knowledge and understanding granted to those who have gone before us in the ministry and work of the gospel, recorded in their writings and expositions.

Almost from the beginning of the preaching of the gospel in the world, God stirred up and enabled many persons to declare by writing what understanding God had given them in and about the meaning of Scripture. Many wrote comments and expositions of many parts of Scripture. And we can see from these writers, both among the Greek and Latin Fathers and among those who have written since the Reformation, how the Holy Spirit divided to them various abilities as he chose. Yet we are free to come to our own judgments about their conclusions. Those who firmly intend to grow in the knowledge of God and of our Lord Jesus Christ will always thank God for the help he gave them in their labours and for the benefit they receive from them.

But concerning all these godly writings I shall only say that the Spirit of God makes them useful and prosperous according to the counsel of his own will. Some misuse them by wandering after their own understanding and corrupting the Word of God. Others go no further than the shell of the text, exercising their skill about words and phrases and expressions, without being led into the spiritual sense of the word concerned, which is its life and power. Others are blessed to a full and proper use of these writings, but only when they fully comply with the spiritual means and duties already described.

10: Final Points on the Work of the Spirit in Relation to Scripture

From what has been said about the work of the Spirit of God in revealing to believers the mind of God in the Scriptures it might seem to follow, firstly, that those who lack this work cannot understand anything of the truth of Scripture, and, secondly, that those who *are* guided by the Spirit must understand the whole of Scripture perfectly.

But both of these conclusions are contrary to experience. Many who apparently lack the saving work of the Spirit, in that no change takes place in their lives, have a great understanding of the truth revealed in Scripture. And many who are truly enlightened and sanctified by the Holy Spirit still fall into many errors and mistakes, as the divisions and differences among Christians openly proclaim. How can this be explained?

1. As to the first point, there are many things in Scripture also found in other writings which any person can come to understand and make a right judgment concerning without any special help from the Holy Spirit.

Also, the main doctrines in Scripture are so plainly and clearly declared that any intelligent person with a little learning and reading can come to a right understanding of them (provided he comes to them without prejudice and bias) without any saving illumination on his mind. This is why it is the fault and sin of all having the use of reason not to see them and assent to them. This is the substance of the Protestant contention against Rome concerning the clarity, or perspicuity, of Scripture, as to its essential doctrines.

Given the natural vanity of the mind of man, its proneness to error and weakness of judgment, we must acknowledge that whatever understanding of the truth it achieves is to be ascribed to the guidance of the Holy Spirit, even when he does not impart saving light and grace. This kind of knowledge of truth is not the Spirit's illumination which we are inquiring into, nor does it renew the mind or conform it in holy obedience to the things seen in Scripture, as saving illumination always does.

2. As to the second point, that those guided by the Spirit should understand the Scripture perfectly, the promise that the Spirit would *teach, instruct, guide and lead into all truth* primarily relates to the great purpose for which God made the revelation: *that we might live to him here according to his will and be brought to enjoy him hereafter in his glory.*

For this purpose, it is not necessary that we should understand the exact sense of every single passage of Scripture or obtain a perfect knowledge of everything in Scripture. It is enough that we come to the knowledge of all truth necessary for the purpose just stated.

This does not absolutely secure us from all errors and mistakes, any more than we are assured of being kept from ever again committing sins. We are not perfectly renewed in this life. The wills of believers are so changed by grace as to guard them from sins inconsistent with a holy life according to the tenor of the covenant of grace, but there is still the possibility of committing many sins.

Similarly the minds of believers are so renewed as to know and assent to all truths necessary to a life of obedience and a right understanding of Scripture, yet the mind is still liable to many mistakes and errors, to our great damage and disadvantage.

Nevertheless, such is the teaching of the Spirit of God, both objectively in Scripture and by the help he gives us through his light and grace, that it is our own *fault*, as well as our *weakness* that we fall into errors and mistakes about any Scripture teaching related to our duty to God.

And if all that believe would freely give up all prejudices and preconceptions and cast off all worldly considerations, giving themselves humbly and entirely to the teaching of God in the ways he has appointed, we might even yet 'all come to the unity of the faith and the knowledge of the Son of God, to a perfect man, to the measure of the stature of the fulness of Christ' (*Eph.* 4:13).

THE SPIRIT'S WATCHFUL CARE OVER THE WRITTEN WORD

There is another important work of the Holy Spirit in relation to Scripture which, though it does not directly concern the saving illumination of believers, yet the whole of what we have said depends on it, as an outward means, and it should be remembered here.

This is *his watchful care over the written Word*, preserving it from destruction and corruption, from the first writing of it to this very day. The entire preservation of the Scriptures despite the opposition it has been exposed to proves his watchful care. But we also have Christ's promise concerning the books of the Old Testament, 'Till heaven and earth pass away, one jot or one tittle will by no means pass from the law till all is fulfilled' (*Matt.* 5:18).

The context shows that 'the law' here means the whole of the Old Testament. And the books of the New are certainly of no less importance and use. From this promise we learn that Scripture will never be *destroyed or abolished*, as a whole or in any necessary part, nor *corrupted*, by changes and falsifications of the copies.

Both of these kinds of attack have been attempted, yet they have failed. Scripture has come through all attacks, not only without *ruin*, but without *wound or blemish*.

This has not been by chance, nor by the care of men alone, but by the special watchful providence and powerful actings of the Spirit of God, in fulfilment of Christ's promise.

Some opinions concerning the integrity and purity of the Scriptures tend to favour the atheistic idea that God has no special regard for his Word and worship in the world. For example, some maintain that books written by inspiration and given to the church as part of its *canon*, or rule of faith and obedience, have been completely lost. Others say that the Old Testament Scriptures have been so corrupted, as to their original letters, that they may and ought to be corrected by translations, especially the Septuagint, or Greek Old Testament. But there is no ground for either of these opinions. And since the integrity and purity of the Scriptures in the original languages may be proved and defended against all opposition, so we must attribute their preservation to the watchful care and powerful operation of the Spirit of God, absolutely securing them throughout all generations.

Part Three

The Holy Spirit and Prayer

1: The Help of the Spirit in Prayer

S ome of the works of the Spirit of God towards believers are general and do not relate to any one duty more
than another. Others relate to some particular duty. The help
which the Spirit gives us in our prayers and supplications is of
the second kind.

Prayer, including meditation, supplication, praise and
thanksgiving, is one of the chief duties in religion. The light of
nature and conscience agree with Scripture in this, that there
cannot be religion in the world without prayer. All who have
acknowledged the existence of God have taught that prayer,
whatever else might accompany it, was the fundamental way
of honouring the God they worshipped.

Prayer, then, is the main and most natural way in which
we converse with God. Without it we are no better than the
beasts which perish. By prayer we make use of all the grace
God has given to us, for by prayer we seek to give to God our
homage and thanks for all his goodness to us.

A person who does not pray is an atheist, for by not praying
he says in his heart, 'There is no God' (*Psa.* 14:1). And yet,
though prayer is generally commended, the evidence of practice, and even the declared opinions of some, give reason to
doubt whether this duty has the acceptance and esteem which
it ought to have.

[89]

However, my purpose in this discourse is not to deal with the nature of prayer in general, the direction Scripture gives in it, or the necessity of its constant use and practice, but only to speak of *the gracious work of the Holy Spirit of God in prayer.*

In Scripture, the work of the Spirit of grace in and towards believers in connection with the duty of prayer is more frequently and expressly asserted than his work in connection with any other grace or duty whatever.

Yet the opposition made in the world against the work of the Spirit in this matter makes it necessary to say something in its vindication. And indeed this is the hinge on which all other differences about the worship of God turn.

The two things I intend to show in the following discourse are these:

1. *That a special work of the Holy Spirit in the prayers and praises of believers is promised and actually granted under the New Testament,* and

2. *What the nature of that work of the Spirit is.*

2: The Spirit of Grace and Supplication: Zechariah 12:10 Expounded

The promise in Zechariah 12:10 that the Holy Spirit, the Spirit of grace and supplication, would be poured out in rich abundance will form the foundation of the discourse which is to follow.

The expression 'pouring out' in connection with the giving of the Spirit shows the abundance of the dispensation promised (*Titus* 3:6). And this promise is specially for the days of the gospel, since the pouring out leads to looking to Christ as pierced, that is, crucified.

The Spirit of grace and supplication is particularly promised to 'the house of David and the inhabitants of Jerusalem'. Here the whole church is symbolized by the ruling family and the people who lived under their rule.

The *house of David* is expressly mentioned, firstly because the faithfulness of God was concerned to preserve that family from which Christ came. Secondly, all the promises in a special manner were to be fulfilled in the person of Christ who was typified by David and his house. The Spirit was first to be poured out on him, then communicated to others. The inhabitants of Jerusalem symbolize the whole church because Jerusalem was the seat of all public ordinances of worship (*Psa.* 122).

The way the promised Spirit is described: Firstly, he is a *Spirit of grace*. *Grace* in the Hebrew and Greek signifies the way in which God deals with sinners in pity, compassion, free goodness and bounty. The word is sometimes used for the grace and favour of God, from which come all his gracious and merciful acts towards us (*Rom.* 1:7; 4:16; 5:2, 15, 20; 6:1, and countless other places).

Grace is also used for the gracious favour of God by which he accepts us in Christ (*Eph.* 2:5; *2 Thess.* 1:12; *Rom.* 16:20; *1 Cor.* 16:23); for the favour of men (*Gen.* 39:4, 21; *1 Sam.* 2:26; *Prov.* 3:4; *Esther* 2:15, 17; 5:2; *Luke* 2:52; *Acts* 4:33); for the free effectual working of grace in those in whom it is (*Acts* 14:26; *1 Cor.* 15:10; *2 Cor.* 12:9); for our justification and salvation by the free grace or favour of God in Christ (*John* 1:17; *1 Pet.* 1:13); for the gospel itself as the means by which the grace of God is declared and brought home to our hearts (*2 Cor.* 6.1; *Eph.* 3:2; *Col.* 1:6; *Titus* 2:11); and for the free giving of the grace and gifts of the Spirit (*John* 1:16; *Eph.* 4:7).

The Spirit may be called the Spirit of grace to show the sovereign cause of his coming, which is the free grace of God (*Titus* 3:4–7). He is also the author of grace in those on whom he is poured out. Again, those who receive him have grace and favour with God. They are 'accepted in the Beloved' (*Eph.* 1:6). In particular he will work grace and holiness in all on whom he is poured out.

Secondly, he is a *Spirit of supplication*, that is, of prayer for grace and mercy. Both 'grace' and 'supplication' are derived from the same Hebrew word which means 'to be gracious or merciful'. The word expresses our approach to God seeking his grace and mercy. 'Supplication' is only used of vocal prayer, either among the people of God or in private.

The Greek word for 'supplication' is used only in Hebrews 5:7. Originally, the word signified a bough or olive branch wrapped with wool or bay leaves. Suppliants carried and lifted up such a branch when they wished to obtain peace or turn away anger. Livy writes of those 'holding olive branches' and other tokens used by suppliants. They prayed that they might be received 'into grace and favour'. Virgil in his *Aeneid* speaks of 'branches of supplication', and he quotes the same Greek word used in the Epistle to the Hebrews.

The Hebrew word for supplication can properly mean nothing but prayers for grace and mercy (*Job* 41:3; *Prov.* 18:23; *Dan.* 9:3, 18, 23; *Jer.* 3:21; 31:9; *2 Chron.* 6:21; *Psa.* 28:2, 6; 31:22; 86:6; 116:1; 130:2; 140:6; 143:1). All these verses indicate disapproval of sin and supplications for grace.

A *Spirit of supplication* is a Spirit abounding in prayer for mercy, but the Holy Spirit has no need to pray for mercy and the turning away of wrath from himself. Nor does he personally pray for us that God will be merciful to us and turn his wrath away from us. This is the priestly work of Christ. Also, to pray to another implies that the suppliant is inferior to the one prayed to. But the Holy Spirit has no nature inferior to the divine. The *Spirit of supplication* must then be the Holy Spirit working in believers to produce gracious inclinations to the duty of prayer, as well as the gracious ability to discharge this duty. Both of these gracious works of the Spirit are summed up by Paul (see *Rom.* 8:26).

God, then, has promised under the New Testament to give to believers richly, the Spirit of grace and supplication, that is, his own Holy Spirit, enabling every believer to pray according to his mind and will.

IS THE PROMISE FOR THE TIME OF THE GOSPEL?

Some object that 'the Spirit of grace and supplication' was given to believers under the Old Testament. Therefore, unless some extraordinary gift is meant, this cannot be a special promise for those under the New Testament. This promise must then refer to some extraordinary gift bestowed on the apostles and first converts to the church. In the same way the prophecy concerning the outpouring of the Spirit on all sorts of persons given by the prophet Joel is interpreted by Peter and applied to the sending of the Holy Spirit in miraculous gifts on the day of Pentecost (*Joel* 2:28–32; *Acts* 2:14–21).

Answer. I have shown elsewhere the foolishness of imagining that the dispensation of the Spirit is confined to the early times of the gospel only. We nowhere find grace and prayer, the things promised here, to be reckoned among the extraordinary gifts of the Spirit under the New Testament. Prayer in an unknown tongue was an extraordinary gift, but ordinary prayer was not. If it was an extraordinary gift, then the present church would be graceless and prayerless.

The promise in Joel referred expressly to the extraordinary gifts of prophecy and visions and therefore had its chief accomplishment on the day of Pentecost. This promise of *the Spirit of grace and supplication* is of another nature altogether. That which is necessary for all believers and the duty of all believers for all times cannot be an extraordinary gift bestowed on a few for a while.

Now if any think that grace and prayer are not necessary to all believers, or that believers may have abilities and be able rightly to use those abilities for the glory of God without the help of the Holy Spirit, I will not at present dispute with them. This is not the place to argue with those who deny the principles of the Christian faith.

If this is not a special promise of the New Testament because the grace promised was in some degree and measure enjoyed under the Old Testament, then there is no promise made concerning prayer for those under the New Testament, for the saints under the Old Testament were in fact made partakers of all the same graces with those under the New.

Two things, therefore, are meant by this promise with respect to the times of the gospel:

1. *The grace of prayer would not be confined to a few as in the Old Testament,* but be given to many and poured out the world over. It would be shed abroad and imparted to many as God's gracious gift to his people.

2. *In gospel times there would be an increase of spiritual abilities for the performance of prayer* (*Titus* 3:5–6). Hence, there is now a rich communication of the Spirit of grace and prayer granted to believers, compared with what was enjoyed under the Old Testament.

There were, indeed, under the Old Testament, prayers and praises to God dictated by a Spirit of prophecy, and received by direct revelation for the instruction of the church in all ages. These prayers were not suggested by the help of the Spirit as the Spirit of supplication, but dictated by the Spirit as the Spirit of prophecy. Nor did the prophets understand the mind of the Spirit in these prayers, but had to study them for themselves, as with all other revelations given to them, and this they did with the help of the Spirit of Christ which was in them (*1 Pet.* 1:10–12). But this gift has ceased under the New Testament and does not belong to our present enquiry.

And even if it could be proved, which I know it cannot, that the generality of the church under the Old Testament made use of any *forms of prayers,* not as means of mystical instruction, but simply to enable them to utter prayer, it does not follow that believers may do the same under the New Testament. Now there is a more plentiful and rich supply of the Spirit of grace and supplication poured out upon us than was poured out under the Old Testament.

God's commands are suited to each dispensation of his grace. Therefore, for those under the New Testament, who are commanded to pray, constantly to reject the help of the promised Spirit of prayer, is to make themselves guilty of the highest ingratitude, even though they claim that it was so done under the Old Testament. We may and ought to bear with them who, not having received anything of this promised grace and help in prayer and not believing that any such promise has been made, use forms of prayer composed by some and read by others or by themselves in order to carry out their duty, yet we who have received the Spirit of grace and supplication will be careful always to look to him for help in prayer, and not admit any principles or practices which in effect deny our need of his help, and so nullify the promise.

Our consideration of this text, then, leads us to this conclusion: *God has promised, under the New Testament, to give the Spirit of grace and supplication, or his own Holy Spirit, to believers in an abundant measure, so enabling them to pray according to his mind and will.*

3: The Spirit of Adoption: Galatians 4:6 Expounded

We come next to the accomplishment of this promise under the New Testament: 'And because you are sons, God has sent forth the Spirit of his Son into your hearts, crying out, "Abba, Father!"' (*Gal.* 4:6).

Those to whom the Spirit is given are believers who, by the Spirit of adoption, have been made children of God. This privilege of adoption is obtained by faith in Jesus Christ (*John* 1:12).

The Spirit is particularly described here as the Spirit of God's Son. He is called this, not only because of his eternal relation to the Son, as proceeding from him, but because he was given to Jesus Christ as head of the church, for the anointing, consecration and sanctification of his human nature. Then from and by Christ he is communicated to us.

The Spirit is given to us by virtue of the covenant between the Father and Christ. Christ, having finished his work of mediation in his state of humiliation and subsequent exaltation to the right hand ofthe Father, 'received the promise of the Holy Spirit'. This means that Christ received the power and authority to give the Holy Spirit to whom he would, for all the purposes of his mediation (*Acts* 2:33; 5:32).

All the graces of the Holy Spirit are received by us from Christ as the head of the church. Christ is the spring of all spiritual life. In him all spiritual graces are treasured up with the express purpose of being dispensed to his people who believe in him (*Col.* 1:19; 2:19; 3:1-4; *Eph.* 4:16).

POWER, LOVE, AND A SOUND MIND (*2 Tim.* 1:7)

As the Spirit of the Son, the Holy Spirit enables believers to conduct themselves agreeably to that state and condition into which they have been taken by faith in Christ Jesus. They are now children of God by adoption and must behave as such. The Spirit teaches them to live no longer as foreigners and strangers, nor as servants only, but as 'children' and as 'heirs of God' (*Rom.* 8:15, 17). He removes the distance, fear, dread and bondage they were subject to (*2 Tim.* 1:7). He is bestowed as the Spirit of power, strengthening and enabling believers to carry out obediently all the duties to which the Father calls his children (*1 Tim.* 1:12). He also gives believers a new heart of love for the Father and a wholehearted desire to be well pleasing to him. As the Spirit of love, he enables them to love God and to delight in him as Father, and as the Spirit of a sound mind, he enables believers to behave themselves with that becoming humility of mind which is honouring to God (*2 Tim.* 1:7; *Rom.* 8:15).

The Spirit enables the sons of God to cry out in prayer, 'Abba, Father'. 'Abba' is the Syriac or Chaldee name for 'father' and was a word in common use among the Jews.

The Jews have a saying in the Babylonian Talmud, in the *Treatise of Blessings*, 'Servants and handmaids (bondslaves), do not call someone Abba or Imma.' Freedom from slavery, with a right to adoption, of which they were incapable, was required for this liberty and confidence.

God gives to his adopted sons 'a free Spirit' (*Psa.* 51:12). This Spirit is a Spirit of gracious, honest, open, frank, sonship. This is the Spirit which cries 'Abba' (*Rom.* 8:15). This is the word by which those who were adopted first greeted their fathers, showing their affection and obedience, for it means not just 'Father' but 'My Father'.

The Holy Spirit enables believers to cry 'Abba, Father' by stirring up their graces, desires and feelings, especially those of faith, love and delight, and by enabling them to exercise those graces and to express those desires in vocal prayer. 'Crying' implies such an earnestness of mind as is expressed in vocal prayer (*Matt.* 27:50).

To cry out to God, 'Abba, Father', is an act of grace and spiritual power wrought in believers by the Holy Spirit alone. But, as a duty performed by us with the Spirit's help, it is also a work of ours. By the inward operation of the Spirit, we are enabled to cry out, 'Abba, Father'. To deny the Spirit's work in enabling us to carry out the duty of prayer is to contradict the express testimony of God and, by our unbelief, to make him a liar.

But the testimony we have been considering is enough to make good our general assertion, *that there is a special gracious work of the Holy Spirit exerted in the prayers of believers enabling them to carry out that duty.*

4: The Nature of Prayer: Romans 8:26 Vindicated

Prayer I understand to be that gift, ability or spiritual skill to exercise faith, love, reverence, fear, delight and other graces in vocal requests, supplications and praises to God (*Phil.* 4:6). This gift and ability is a real, gracious effect and work of the Holy Spirit of God.

The first thing we ascribe to the Spirit is to provide us with a due understanding of *the matter of prayer*, or what we should pray for (*Rom.* 8:26). Without this there can be no prayer, for how can anyone pray who does not know what to pray for?

But this is the express testimony of the Apostle in Romans 8:26, that we do not know what we should pray for as we ought, without the special assistance of the Spirit. It is one thing to have what we ought to pray for in Scripture, another to have it in our minds and hearts. There is a threefold defect in us with respect to the matter of prayer.

THE MATTER OF PRAYER

1. *We do not know our real needs.* As to our outward situations, pressures and difficulties, great wisdom is needed to make these a matter of prayer according to the mind of God (*Eccles.* 6:12). Our knowledge of our inward needs is also very dark and confused without the aid of the Spirit. Natural conscience will not suffice.

As for our inward spiritual habits and attitudes of soul and how they are worked upon by grace and by sin, we need to be searched by God (*Psa.* 139:23–24). God requires truth in the inward parts. We need wisdom to know what is going on in the inward parts. It is for this wisdom that the Psalmist prays (*Psa.* 51:6). It is the inward sanctification of all our faculties (*1 Thess.* 5:23) for which we ought to pray. We need continuous supplies of grace for this. We need a sense of the power, guilt, violence and deceit of sin as it attempts to rule and control our minds and hearts. We need to know what in us is displeasing to God. We need to know and acknowledge God's wisdom, grace and love in Christ Jesus, with all the fruits, effects and blessings which we receive. We need to know what hinders or helps our access to the throne of grace.

In order to manage all these things rightly in our prayers, we need the help of the Spirit of grace and supplication.

2. *We do not know the real bearing of the promises of God on our needs.* All that God has promised and nothing else should be the subject matter of our prayers. We must pray according to his will. But these are spiritual things and must be spiritually discerned. We cannot understand them without the special help of the Spirit of God.

3. *We do not rightly understand the motives we should have in prayer.* It is possible to ask and not receive because we ask for the wrong reasons (*James* 4:3). If we are left to ourselves, our aims will never be suited to the will of God. There is nothing so excellent in itself, so useful to us, so acceptable to God, in the matter of prayer, but that it may be corrupted and the prayer made useless because we pray for the wrong reasons and from the wrong motives. The work of the Spirit to guide us in the matter of prayer will be considered in the next chapter.

5: The Spirit Teaches Us What to Pray For

The first work of the Spirit as a Spirit of supplication in believers is to give them an understanding of their real needs and of the supplies of grace and mercy laid up in the promises of God. Without this men never pray, and with it, in a sense, they are always praying.

I will give some instances of the understanding of our needs and of the relief of them which the Spirit gives.

FAITH AND UNBELIEF

The apostles prayed, 'Lord, increase our faith.' A poor man in his distress prayed, 'Lord, help my unbelief.'

I cannot believe that anyone prays aright who never prays for the pardon and removal of unbelief and for the increase of faith. If unbelief is the greatest of sins and faith the greatest of God's gifts, we are not Christians if these things are not prominent in our prayers. We must be convinced of the nature and guilt of unbelief and the nature and use of faith. That this is the special work of the Holy Spirit our Saviour clearly declares, 'He will convince the world of sin, because they do not believe in me' (*John* 16:8–9). Not believing in Jesus Christ is a sin against the gospel and it is by the gospel alone, ministered to us by the Holy Spirit, that we may be convinced of it. Neither the light of natural conscience nor the law will convince anyone of the guilt of not believing in Jesus Christ, nor teach them the true nature of faith in him.

To teach men to pray without a sense of unbelief in its guilt and power or without any idea of the true nature of faith is to say to the naked and hungry, 'Be warmed and filled', and not give them those things that are needful to the body.

If the things which are of the greatest importance to us and on which our eternal salvation hangs are not a chief part of the subject matter of our daily prayers, I do not know what deserves to be.

THE DEPRAVITY OF OUR NATURE

If we are to pray aright we need a knowledge of and a due sense of the depravity of our nature and our need to be delivered from it. But human nature is so corrupted as not to understand its own depravity. It is blind to this, too proud to admit it, too senseless to feel it. It is the work of the Spirit of God alone to give a spiritual insight into these things, and without this I cannot see how men can pray.

And as it is with sin, so it is with respect to God and Christ, and the covenant of grace, holiness and privileges. We have no spiritual conceptions of these, no right understanding of them, but what is given to us by the Spirit of God. Without an acquaintance with these things, what are our prayers worth? What do they signify? Without them we may utter words to the world's end without giving any glory to God or obtaining any advantage for our souls. Ignorance of this is the reason why some reproach and vilify the aid of the Spirit in prayer. Our differences with them will not be resolved by argument, but only by a more plentiful pouring out of the Spirit of God.

GRACE AND MERCY IN THE PROMISES

We do not know what to pray for as we ought, but the Holy Spirit makes known to us the grace and mercy prepared in the promises of God for our relief. What is the purpose of our prayers? What answers do we expect to obtain? Praying

[103]

only by repeating words without any understanding of what we are praying for or why we are praying is unworthy of the disciples of Christ or indeed of rational creatures. 'Offer it then to your governor! Would he be pleased with you? Would he accept you favourably?' (*Mal.* 1:8). No ruler or friend or neighbour would be pleased with us if we merely repeated set forms of words and speeches to them with no reason or purpose in mind.

We must 'pray with our understanding', that is, understand what we are praying for and why. The things we pray for are the things God has promised to give us. If we do not pray for these we 'ask amiss'. It is therefore absolutely necessary that we should know what God has promised and have an understanding of the grace and mercy contained in these promises.

God knows what is good for us, what is useful to us, what is necessary to bring us to the full enjoyment of himself, infinitely better than we do ourselves. In fact we know nothing of these things but what he is pleased to teach us. These are the things God has 'prepared for us' (*1 Cor.* 2:9). What God has prepared for us he tells us in the promises of his covenant, for they declare the grace and good pleasure which he has purposed in himself.

The reason why so many are so barren in their prayers and make so many repetitions of the same requests, is because they are ignorant of the promises of God and the grace that is in them.

How then are we to become acquainted with these promises? By the Spirit of God, without whose help we can neither understand the promises nor see what is contained in them. Admittedly, some, with only the help of a good memory, may be able to plead the promises of God in their prayers, but they lack a spiritual acquaintance with the grace wrapped up in the promises. They may well minister to others, but they cannot minister to their own souls.

However, the Spirit opens the eyes of believers; he gives them understanding; he enlightens their minds so that they can see the things that are prepared for them by God. He displays these things which God has prepared for believers in all their beauty, glory, suitability and desirability. He makes them see Christ and all the fruits of his mediation in the promises. He shows believers the grace and love of God in them.

When the mind and heart are continually filled with the things that God has prepared for those that love him, they will never lack matter for prayer.

FORMS OF PRAYER

Objection: 'If men are unacquainted with the promises of God, and so do not know what they ought to pray for, others who are acquainted with these things may compose prayers for them which they can have ready for use at any time.'

Answer: I do not know of any command given by God for the composition of prayers, nor of any promise of divine help to enable men to compose prayers for the use of others. The Spirit of grace and supplication is promised to enable us to pray, not to enable us to compose prayers for others.

A person must be unacquainted with the promises of God and the duty of prayer to imagine that he can compose a prayer suitable for all the various conditions of believers. Much of what we are to pray about may be put into a form of words, as they are in the Lord's Prayer, which gives directions in prayer and keeps our requests in bounds. But to think that we can compose detailed prayers to suit the needs of those who are to pray is foolish. There is a vast difference between

[105]

showing people what they ought to pray for and giving them a love and desire for those things. The latter is the work of the Spirit.

Those who use forms of prayer composed by others will still not understand the spiritual import of the things for which they pray unless the Holy Spirit gives them spiritual understanding. He gives believers such an understanding of promised grace and mercy that they are enabled to apply these promises to their daily needs in prayer, praise and thanksgiving. But when a person is made to pray by forms not applicable to their present state and condition, there is spiritual confusion and disorder, and nothing else.

THE COMMANDS OF GOD

What has been said about the promises of God must also be applied to the commands of God. These also provide matter for our prayers, both in confession and in supplication. But without a right understanding of God's commands we cannot pray as we ought.

His commands are spiritual and inward. And we cannot have a spiritual understanding of the law but by the enlightening grace of the Holy Spirit. Where this is, the mind is greatly supplied with matter for prayer. The Spirit alone can display the law in all its glory and show us how far short of it we have fallen.

INTENTIONS IN PRAYER

The Spirit alone can direct and guide believers to pray for anything for the right reasons. To pray for the wrong reasons is to render our prayers useless. But the Spirit 'makes intercession for the saints according to the will of God' (*Rom.* 8:27). This means that he enables us to make intercession according to the will of God. What the Spirit does in this respect, he does in and by us. He therefore directs and enables us to make supplications 'according to the will of God'. By the supplications which the Spirit enables us to make, God is said to 'know the mind of the Spirit', that is, God approves of and accepts the Spirit's intention in the requests he enables us to make.

But there may be, and I believe there is, more in that expression, 'God knows the mind of the Spirit'. The Holy Spirit works such high, holy spiritual desires and purposes in the minds of believers in their supplications that God alone knows and understands their full extent and breadth.

I will mention two general ways in which the Spirit guides the motives or intentions of our prayers:

1. *He guides us to direct all our prayers to the glory of God.* He alone enables us to subordinate all our desires to God's glory. Without this we would ultimately aim at self in everything, and this would spoil our prayers and make them abominable.

2. He also keeps us to this, *that we should aim in everything we ask at the advancement of holiness and conformity to God.* Without these objectives, the matter of prayer might be right and according to the Word of God, and yet our prayers be an abomination.

And this is the first part of the work of the Spirit of God towards believers as a Spirit of grace and supplication, filling their minds with matter for prayer and thereby teaching them what to pray for as they ought.

6: The Spirit Teaches Us How to Pray

We have considered the *matter* of prayer, but we must also consider the due *manner* in which we should pray. The Holy Spirit not only shows to our minds the things we ought to pray for, but he also gives to our wills and affections a due sense of the value of these things. The mind may have light to know what to pray for, but the will and affections may be dead or unconcerned about them. However, prayer, properly so called, is the soul submitting itself obediently to the will of God. Therefore the Spirit not only enables us to pray, but he also works in us feelings and desires appropriate to that for which we are praying.

RIGHT FEELINGS AND DESIRES

It is the Holy Spirit who enables us to pray with deep feeling and earnest desire. He stirs up within us 'groanings which cannot be uttered' (*Rom.* 8:26–27). He works in us such intense desires and labouring of mind that natural affections cannot approach to them.

He also so enlightens the mind in the truth, beauty and excellency of spiritual things as to produce a love to, delight in and choice of these things, and a holy, supernatural desire and endeavour after union with them, in the enjoyment of them.

To evade the force of the words in Romans 8:26–27, some have taken it to refer to the intercession of the Spirit in Christ now at the right hand of God, but this sense is not appropriate, either to the present, glorious condition of the Mediator or to the words themselves.

What is wrought in the hearts of believers by the Holy Spirit as they fulfil their duty of prayer, none but he who searches the hearts can know. These supernatural, holy desires are what we ought to aim at, especially in times when we are most aware of our infirmities and weaknesses. Indeed, we are always to endeavour after these workings of grace in all our prayers.

DELIGHT IN GOD

The Holy Spirit also gives the soul of a believer a delight in God as the one to whom we pray. Without this delight, the duty of prayer is not accepted with God and is a barren, burdensome task. Delight in God includes:

1. *A sight of God as on a throne of grace* (*Heb.* 11:27; 4:6), not by carnal imagination but by spiritual illumination. God seen on a throne of grace is God ready, through Jesus Christ, to give grace and mercy to sinners who seek him.

The throne of grace is set up in the most holy place which the high priest alone could enter once a year, and only with the blood of the sacrifice. But now the way into the most holy presence of God has been opened to all believers. We have 'boldness to enter into the holiest by the blood of Jesus' (*Heb.* 10:19) and are encouraged to 'come boldly to the throne of grace, that we may obtain mercy and find grace to help in time of need' (*Heb.* 4:16).

God as a Judge is not seen on a throne of grace (see *Dan.* 7:9–10). If a sinner comes to God seated on the throne of judgment he will feel nothing but dread and terror and will foolishly try to avoid him and his displeasure (*Isa.* 33:14; *Mic.* 6:6–7; *Rev.* 6:16–17).

The Holy Spirit, therefore, brings us rather to the throne of grace. 'Therefore the LORD will wait, that he may be gracious to you; and therefore he will be exalted, that he may have mercy on you' (*Isa.* 30:18). Without this assurance that God will be gracious and merciful to us, we cannot draw near to him or call upon him with delight, like children crying 'Abba, Father'.

And this is produced in us by the Holy Spirit alone, who, in and through Christ, reveals the grace of God to us. This is what Paul prays for in his letter to the Ephesians (*Eph.* 1:17–18). By the Spirit, God says to us that 'fury is not in him', and that if we lay hold on his strength to make peace with him, we shall have peace (*Isa.* 27:4–5).

2. *A sense of God's relation to us as a Father* (*2 Cor.* 6:18; *Eph.* 2:18; *Rom.* 8:16). God is not ashamed to be called our Father, and the Lord Jesus, when he taught his disciples to pray, told them to say, 'Our Father'. Therefore God as Father is the highest object of all evangelical worship and of all our prayers. No tongue can express, no mind can reach, the heavenly calmness and soul-satisfying delight indicated by the Apostle's words, 'Through Christ we have access by one Spirit unto the Father.' How full of sweetness and satisfaction this is! Without a right sense of God in this relation to us we cannot pray as we ought. And our only sense of this is by the Spirit, for it is 'the Spirit that bears witness with our spirit that we are the children of God' (*Rom.* 8:16), and this gives us the highest assurance of our sonship that we can have in this world. He is the Spirit of adoption, and it is by him alone that we have any interest in that great privilege.

This has more to do with the duty of prayer than some will admit. There is nothing more essential in prayer than that we come to God as our Father. He is the Father of our Lord Jesus Christ, and in him our Father also. Our only real sense of this is by the Spirit.

3. *A boldness in our access into the holy place, or to the throne of grace (Heb.* 10:19, 22). Where men have a 'spirit of bondage . . . to fear', they can never have any delight in approaching God. This is removed by the Spirit of grace and supplication, the Spirit of adoption, so that we cry 'Abba, Father', and can pray as we ought (*Rom.* 8:15). 'Where the Spirit of the Lord is, there is liberty' (*2 Cor.* 3:17). This consists of two things: *enlarged liberty in speaking to God in prayer*, and *confidence of being heard and accepted.*

The word *boldness* used in this connection means a freedom to speak all that is to be spoken, according to our state and needs. Where this Spirit of liberty and boldness is, the heart is enlarged with a genuine openness to express all its concerns to God as a child to its father. We are enabled to do as the Apostle says, 'Be anxious for nothing, but in everything by prayer and supplication, with thanksgiving, let your requests be made known to God' (*Phil.* 4:6).

All our concerns in this world must be taken to God in prayer. We should not be burdened with anxieties. We must not hide anything from God, which we attempt to do when we do not go to him in prayer. When we bring all our concerns to him, 'the peace of God, which surpasses all understanding, will guard [our] hearts and minds through Jesus Christ' (*Phil.* 4:7.).

There is also the *confidence of being heard and accepted.* Without this we can have no delight in prayer, or in the God to whom we pray. When Adam thought there was no acceptance with God for him, he went and hid himself. And all those who have no ground of spiritual confidence that they are accepted in Christ also seek to hide themselves, even though they pray. They have no delight or enlargement or liberty in praying. Their prayer only creates a mist and obscurity between themselves and God.

[111]

This confidence and boldness is not so much that any particular request we make will be granted, but that God is well pleased with our duties, accepts us and is delighted when we approach him on his throne of grace.

Whatever presumption and superstition may say, sinners naturally see God as hard and incapable of condescension or compassion. They also limit God, saying, 'Can God do this or that thing? Can he really supply our needs?' If these thoughts prevail in us we cannot have any delight in coming to God. But we are freed from them by the Spirit, who shows us the goodness and power of God in the promises of the covenant, and so gives us boldness to enter into his presence with joy.

PRAYING THROUGH CHRIST THE MEDIATOR

Finally, it is the work of the Spirit to *fix our attention on Jesus Christ as the only way and means of acceptance with God*. We are to ask in Christ's name. We enter into the holiest by the new and living way that Christ has consecrated for us. It is by him that 'we have access by one Spirit to the Father' (*Eph.* 2:18; see also *Rom.* 5:2).

The Holy Spirit glorifies Christ as the only way to God in the hearts of believers (*John* 16:14; 14:6). By keeping our hearts and minds close to Christ as Mediator the Spirit refreshes our souls and makes our approaches to God in prayer not burdensome but delightful.

7: The Duty of Praying in the Spirit: Ephesians 6:18 Expounded

The duty I am seeking to describe is what is expressed in Ephesians 6:18: 'Praying always with all prayer and supplication in the Spirit, being watchful to this end with all perseverance and supplication for all the saints'.

PRAYING IN THE SPIRIT

It is our duty to 'pray in the Spirit'. Some have said that this means praying by virtue of an extraordinary or miraculous gift of the Spirit, but this duty is here urged on all Christians and not just a few who were for a time endowed with extraordinary, miraculous gifts. Paul expressly confines the extraordinary gifts to certain times and certain circumstances when they may be useful for edification (*1 Cor.* 14).

There is, therefore, a 'praying in the Spirit' which is the constant duty of believers, and it is a great reproach to the profession of Christianity whenever such praying is held in contempt. If 'praying in the Spirit' is, as some say, foolish, conceited and fanatical, their quarrel is not with us but with Paul. But if 'praying in the Spirit' is a duty which God requires from us, I would not willingly be among those who deride it.

The text also requires believers to pray 'always', or at all times and seasons, 'with all prayer and supplication'. The believer is to pray all kinds of prayers according as the occasion and his needs require. With such a rule before him, how can the believer confine his prayers to a prescribed form of words? Written prayers cannot vary in form and so cannot be suited to all needs and occasions.

I do not conclude that all written forms are unlawful, but only that a different way of praying is here urged on us. If anyone, by written forms only, can do what this text requires, I shall say no more, but they have managed to do what is incomprehensible to me.

Our question is this. How are those in whose minds the Spirit works as a Spirit of grace and supplication enabled to pray? I answer, they are generally enabled to pray aloud to God, as required by their differing circumstances. This is what is called *the gift of prayer*. There may be times of temptation and desertion when they can only 'mourn as a dove' or 'chatter as a crane', that is mourn and groan in brokenness of spirit. But even this is acceptable with God.

Those who confine themselves to a form of words are strangers to the true nature of prayer and the work of the Spirit in it. Then prayer becomes monotonous, with no harmony or music in it.

ACCEPTABLE PRAYER

What, then, is involved in acceptable prayer? I say, first that the things we have described are necessary in some degree and measure to all acceptable prayer.

We are not talking here about prayers wrung from the natural man in difficulties when he prays to the God of nature, showing his dependence on his Creator and acknowledging his power. In this sense, all flesh, at one time or other, come to God in prayer. Nor do we mean prayers wrung from men by legal convictions. What we are dealing with is the kind of prayer required of believers under the gospel. And what I maintain is that those in whom this work is accomplished by the Holy Spirit in any degree do not ordinarily lack the ability to express themselves in vocal prayer so far as is needful. This ability can grow and improve with exercise. It is, therefore, sinful and foolish not to make progress in this ability by stirring up the gifts and graces we have.

Although the use of set forms of prayer may be *lawful* to some, as is claimed, yet they are never *necessary*. Every child of God will be able to pray according to the mind and will of God if he does not neglect the help offered to him for that purpose.

Therefore to plead for the necessity of forms of prayer, beyond what may be doctrinal or instructive in them, comes from party spirit or ignorance or lack of attention to men's own experience.

PRAYER AND THE UNREGENERATE

Are forms of prayer useful to the unregenerate? These are of two kinds. Some are openly under the power of sin and not moved by any convictions. They seldom pray unless in danger, troubles, pains or distresses. When smitten they will cry to God as the sailors did on Jonah's ship (*Jon.* 1:5–6). How can any forms of prayer help them then? How can set prayers express their agonies of heart on such occasions? They would only become superstitious charms said to avert the danger. The substance of the sailors' prayer in Jonah's ship was, 'Think upon us that we may not perish.' Men in such a condition need no set forms of prayer to help them. And crying to God in such a way may impress their minds with a reverence for him and an awareness of their own inability. A set form of prayer would only stifle an awakened conscience and lead men back to their former security.

Other unregenerate persons have a sense of the authority of God's Word and their duty to pray. These will pray conscientiously and carry out other duties which they think will make them acceptable to God. We will say more on this when we deal with forms of prayer later.

But can it be said that these persons cannot express their own minds, so far as they are affected by the things they pray about? Laziness or neglect may keep them in a sense of disability in this matter, but since prayer in this sort of person is an effect of common illumination and common grace, which are also from the Spirit of God, the Spirit will help them to express themselves so far as is necessary for them. Those who never enter the water except with floats and arm-bands will never learn to swim. The constant use of set forms of prayer may be a great means of quenching the Spirit and hindering all further progress.

8: The Spirit Enables Us to Pray Aloud

Until now we have been concerned mainly with the internal, spiritual nature of prayer. But we must also consider prayer as an external performance. It is the will of God that in assemblies which he has appointed, such as churches, families and occasional meetings of two or three or more in the name of Christ, one should pray and the rest should join with him.

PRAYER AS AN OUTWARD GIFT

What we affirm is: *The Holy Spirit enables men to express in suitable words the matter of prayer, as discussed earlier, in such a way as to lead their own and others' minds to communion with God in this duty, to the honour of God and their own edification.* This ability is not confined to public gatherings. Everyone may make use of it in private also. Because many object to what we assert, I will make some observations about it to prepare the way for a clear statement of it.

1. *Every man is to pray or call upon God according to his ability, taking account of his own condition, circumstances and duties.* All who believe in a deity confess that it is their duty to pray to him in words of their own, as well as they are able.

Mere repetition of a *paternoster*, an *ave* or a *credo* with no thought of the words is not prayer, but the taking of God's name in vain and a profanation of a holy ordinance. There has been no more effectual way of bringing unholiness and ungodly behaviour into the Christian world than this of teaching men to satisfy themselves that they truly pray when they say, read or repeat the words of other men. They may not understand the words they use. They are certainly not moved by a sense of their importance. Our whole obedience to God ought to be our 'reasonable service' (*Rom.* 12:1). But prayer cannot be a reasonable service when it is founded on the irrational idea that men should pray, not in their own words, but in the words of others, which they may not even understand.

2. *All examples of prayer in Scripture consist of men's expressing, according to their own ability, the gracious ideas formed in their minds by the Spirit of God.* They never involve the use of forms of words composed by others.

3. *None of the commands to pray given in the Scriptures involve the use of outward prescribed forms or helps.* They all require prayer to come from the ability a person has been given.

4. *When we speak of men's own ability, we do not exclude the use of all means to improve this ability.* These include diligently searching our hearts to know their true state and condition before God. David prays that God would search and try him (*Psa.* 139:23–24). He who would have his prayers to be appropriate, useful and fervent must be diligent in *searching and knowing his own heart* with all its tendencies and desires, and the secret guilt it may contract. *Diligent reading of the Scripture* is another duty on which ability in prayer greatly depends.

5. *Natural abilities of imagination, memory and speech may be made use of in prayer.* And in this regard abilities differ. All men who have the gift of prayer do not all pray in the same way. Some greatly excel others in one respect or another. But in all cases the exercise of these abilities in prayer depends on the special assistance of the Spirit of God.

6. *Spiritual gifts are of two kinds.* Some are distinct from all other abilities, such as the extraordinary gifts of miracles, healings,

tongues and the like. Others are based on something else, as the gift of utterance depends on wisdom and knowledge. Prayer is of this second kind.

Since utterance is an inseparable part of prayer as we have described it, it too is from the Spirit, the author of prayer and everything necessary to it. The whole of prayer, therefore, is a gift of the Spirit. The grace of prayer and the gift of prayer are inseparable.

THE GRACE AND GIFT OF PRAYER

Someone may object: Can it really be true that everyone who has a gracious disposition to pray also has the gift of utterance, or that everyone who has the gift of utterance also has a gracious disposition to pray? Is this not contrary to all experience?

In answer I would say, what we are speaking of here is the grace of prayer in actual exercise. All those in whom the Spirit of God graciously works faith, love, delight in God and a desire for him have also the ability to express themselves aloud in prayer.

It is the duty of Christians to stir up this gift of prayer by constant and frequent use (*2 Tim.* 1:6). But where this duty is neglected it is not surprising if any persons who may have, as they say, the grace of prayer, should not yet have the ability to speak out their minds and desires in prayers in their own words. Some are led to believe that none have this ability to pray out loud and so do not look for it in themselves. Some despise any free expression in prayer. What help such persons may have from the Spirit of grace I do not know. It is not likely that they will receive much help from him if they despise his work. Some are so used to reading prayers from set forms composed by men that they never try to pray for themselves. A child brought up among none but those who walk with crutches may well refuse to walk except with crutches. But good instruction, or an emergency of some kind, may make him use his own strength and throw away the needless help. Similarly Christians may fail to use the gracious ability they have, until the right circumstances call it forth.

The ability we are speaking of is not absolute but suited to the needs and conditions of the person. Each has his own ability according to his need. If God calls us to higher positions and duties in the church, he will give us greater ability, suitable to our circumstances.

As to the objection that all who have the gift of praying aloud must also have the grace of prayer, and this is certain evidence that they have received saving grace, I say, this does not follow. Grace gives birth to the gift, but the gift and ability to pray aloud may come from a common work of illumination. Men in whom the Spirit of grace does not savingly reside may have the gift and ability to speak in prayer to the edification of themselves and others. However, to suppose that a man could have a gift of prayer without illumination is to suppose that he may pray when he has no idea what to pray for. This would be the kind of mindless fanaticism which we abhor.

PRAYER NOT COMPLETE WITHOUT WORDS

The duty of prayer is usually not complete unless it is expressed in words. In Scripture prayer is called, 'pleading with God', 'filling our mouth with arguments', 'crying to him', and 'causing him to hear our voice'. Such praying is not needful to God, but it is needful to us.

It may be said that all this may be done by internal meditation where no use is made of the voice or words. Hannah 'spoke in her heart; only her lips moved, but her voice was not heard' (*1 Sam.* 1:13). In some cases this may be so. Some circumstances call for inward, silent prayer, as do some strong, violent feelings, which cause men to cry out. But in this prayer of meditation, the mind still expresses itself in words and expressions even though they are not uttered. Hannah said of herself, 'Out of the abundance of my complaint and grief I have spoken' (verse 16). She not only put her thoughts and desires into words and phrases but also expressed them to God silently within herself. Her mind was fully active in inward, silent prayers.

UTTERANCE A GIFT OF THE SPIRIT

Utterance is a special gift of the Holy Spirit (*1 Cor.* 1:5; *2 Cor.* 8:7; *Eph.* 6:19; *Col.* 4:3), exercised both in speaking to men in the name of God, in preaching the Word, and in speaking to God for ourselves and others.

It is the ability to speak out boldly and freely what is in our minds, and in sacred things, in praying and preaching, it is the gift of the Holy Spirit. We are to pray for this gift for ourselves or others since the spiritual edification of the church depends on it. The foundation of the church was laid in it, as an extraordinary gift (*Acts* 2:4), and now the building up of the church continues through it. Utterance is the sole means of public intercourse between God and his church.

It is the Spirit who enables men to carry out every duty required of them in the right way, and without his help we can do nothing as we should.

This is true of ministers of the gospel as they fulfil their ministry in prayer and preaching (*1 Tim.* 2:1; *Acts* 6:4; *Eph.* 4:12). Utterance is the gift of the Spirit to them and in them. Any who are destitute of this gift cannot carry out the duties of a minister of the gospel. If a spiritual ability to pray and preach is not essential to the office of the ministry, then what is?

Utterance is also involved in the duties of those in other callings, such as parents and heads of families who pray with their families as well as for them.

This gift is so spiritually beneficial for the building up of Christians individually, of Christian families, and especially of churches, that it would be impious not to attribute it to the working of the Spirit. Experience shows that it is not merely a matter of natural ability improved by practice. And without that illumination of the mind which is a special gift of the Spirit, no-one attains the ability to pray.

Thus I have delineated the work of the Holy Spirit as a Spirit of grace and supplication, promised to and bestowed on all believers, enabling them to cry, 'Abba, Father'. Next we shall consider how we may best make use of what we have learned, in our life of obedience to God.

9: Our Response to the Gift of the Spirit of Prayer

'If we know these things, happy are we if we do them', and not otherwise. How should we respond to the free gift of God's grace, of which we have been speaking?

First, we ought constantly to give glory to God for it. Secondly, we should attend constantly to the duty which we are graciously enabled to perform through this gift.

GIVING GLORY TO GOD FOR HIS GIFT

We ought continually to praise God and give glory to him for this great privilege of the Spirit of grace and supplication granted to the church.

Without this gift, the world gropes in the dark and wanders after vain ideas, not knowing how to pray to God about all its concerns and convictions. Those who despise, revile and blaspheme this gift, and hide themselves from the light, do not know what they are doing, or by what spirit they are led. Our duty is to pray that God would pour out his Spirit on them also. Then he would quickly cause them to 'look on him whom they have pierced, and mourn'.

Two things show how great a mercy and privilege it is to have this gift. Firstly, a psalmist and a prophet both pray directly and without any qualification that God would 'pour out his fury on the families that call not on his name' (*Psa.* 79:6; *Jer.* 10:25). Secondly, the whole of our obedience in faith is involved in this duty of prayer (*Rom.* 10:13). In Scripture, *calling on God* is used to signify our whole worship of God and obedience of faith. No heart can fully grasp the treasury of mercies which lies in this one privilege of having liberty and ability to approach God at all times, according to his mind and will, by this Spirit of grace and supplication. This provides all the church's comfort, all her security.

It is a particular cause of praise and glory to God that this privilege is so much enlarged under the gospel. The difference between the Old Testament and the New does not lie only in the outward letter, ceremonies and rituals. Some who love ceremonies and rituals, whose religion lies only in the letter of the law, might prefer the Old Testament to the plainness and simplicity of the gospel. But those who know what it is to 'receive the Spirit of adoption by whom we cry "Abba, Father"', and what it is to 'serve God in the newness of the Spirit and not in the oldness of the letter', well understand the difference.

Also, under the gospel this grace is now communicated to multitudes, whereas under the Old Testament it was confined to a few. Then the dew of the Spirit watered only the land of Canaan and the posterity of Abraham according to the flesh. Now showers are poured down on all nations, on 'all that in every place call on the name of Jesus Christ our Lord'. This is done in fulfilment of that great promise in Malachi, 'For from the rising of the sun, even to its going down, my name shall be great among the Gentiles; in every place incense shall be offered to my name, and a pure offering; for my name shall be great among the nations, says the Lord of hosts' (*Mal.* 1:11). All the glory and beauty of our assemblies and worship lies in the fruits and effects of the works of the Spirit.

The Spirit is the same to believers all over the world, in their private rooms or their prisons. All have 'access by one Spirit to the Father' (*Eph.* 2:18). And in return for this enlargement of grace, God rightly expects a return of glory from us.

MAKING USE OF THE GIFT OF THE SPIRIT

1. *It is our duty to make use of the gift of the Spirit, which was bought for us by Christ and is of priceless value to our souls.* There are two ways in which we may be guilty of neglecting this heavenly gift. We neglect it when we do not value it, seek it, or make every effort to obtain it. We neglect this gift also when we do not constantly and diligently make use of it to fulfil the purpose for which God gave it.

Do you have an ability to pray always, freely given to you by the Holy Spirit? Why then do you not always pray, in private, in your families and whenever you have opportunity?

There are so many hindrances and difficulties in the way of prayer. What discouragements rise up against it. What an aversion to prayer has corrupt nature. What distractions and weariness we find when we pray. Yet our eternal happiness and our present comforts and joys so much depend upon it. Who can fully describe the foolishness and the sinfulness of neglecting this gift of prayer? Can we grieve the Holy Spirit more, and more effectively damage our own souls than by neglecting to pray? Is not this the way to 'quench the Spirit'? How shall we answer for the contempt of this gracious help offered us by Jesus Christ?

Shall others at the tinkling of a bell rise and run to prayers to be said or sung, prayers in which they have no spiritual interest, said only to quiet their consciences and satisfy their prejudices, and shall we neglect that spiritual help which has so graciously been given to us? Will not the blind devotion and superstition of multitudes rise up in judgment against us if we neglect this privilege and grace? Having lost the Spirit of God, they have invented many ways to keep up the appearance of prayer. And shall we who have received that Spirit which the world cannot receive be treacherous and disobedient to his promptings and leadings? Who can express the horrible ingratitude of such a sin?

I press this particularly because the temptations and dangers of the days we live in especially call for it. If we would talk less and pray more, things would be better than they are in the world. At least we should be enabled to bear them better and be better prepared to meet whatever we are called to go through.

2. *If we have received this gift, it is our duty to cherish it, to stir it up and to make better use of it.* It is freely given and it must be carefully kept. Several things will be helpful to us in this respect:

i. *A constant consideration and observation of ourselves, our own hearts and our spiritual state and condition (Psa. 16:7; 19:12; 139:23–24).* About such things as we find, we are to deal with God in our supplications (*Phil.* 4:6).

ii. *Constant searching of the Scriptures for the same purpose.* This is the mirror in which we may take the best view of ourselves, showing us both what we are and what we ought to be. We should turn what we read into praise or prayer to God. We have an example of this in Psalm 119 where every consideration of God's will and our duty is turned into a petition.

iii. *Meditation on God's glorious excellencies.* This will help us greatly to cherish his gracious gift of the Holy Spirit. It will stir up in us that reverence and godly fear which is required by all that draw near to this infinitely holy God (*Lev.* 10:3; *Heb.* 12:28) and greatly encourage us in prayer (*Heb.* 10:19–22; 4:6). It will rouse up within us faith and confidence, so that we go to God as our shield, our rock, and our reward (*Prov.* 18:10; *Gen.* 15:1).

iv. *Meditation on the mediation and intercession of Christ* will encourage us to pray (*Heb.* 4:15–16; 10:19–22). By this we can test whether our faith is truly evangelical or not. Some say that the eagle tests the eyes of her young by turning them to the sun. If they cannot look steadily at the sun, she rejects them as spurious. We can test our faith by the Sun of righteousness. If ours is a true faith it will look steadily at Christ. But if it turns away from Christ and looks to other things it is spurious. A false faith cannot look steadily on the Person and mediation of Christ.

v. *Frequent use of prayer* will greatly strengthen and improve this gift, as use of any gift does (*1 Cor.* 12:7; *1 Pet.* 4:10, 11), whereas neglect can lead to a gift being withdrawn (*Matt.* 25:29). This is the eternal law concerning the gifts of God's grace.

vi. *Constant fervency and intentness of mind and spirit* in this duty works towards the same end. Many prayers, uttered in a dull, dead and lazy manner, will not achieve this. Fervency and intentness cast the whole soul into the mould of the things we are praying for and prepare us for fresh spiritual engagement with them. Fervency should not be confused with vehemency or loudness, however. Loudness is only justified when we have to be heard by a large gathering, or when our vehement feelings will bear no restraint (*Psa.* 22:1; *Heb.* 5:7).

All these things both help to cherish, preserve and improve the gift of prayer, and are themselves the ways in which grace, and the work of the Spirit of supplication, exert themselves in our prayers.

3. *Our duty is to use this gift of prayer for the purpose for which it was freely given to us.* And this respects both those who receive the gift and those others who will benefit from it. As to those who receive the gift, it is a blessed means to stir up, excite and quicken into activity all those graces of the Spirit by which we have communion with God in the duty of prayer. These

include faith, love, delight, joy and the like. In prayer the mind and soul are fixed on the things which are the proper objects of these graces. Formal prayers cannot achieve this. True prayer alone stirs up the graces and holy affections on whose working the life and efficacy of this duty consists.

Praying aloud increases the fervour and efficacy of our prayers. Expressing our desires in our own words stirs up our hearts further for the satisfaction of those desires. Therefore vocal, audible prayer is generally more profitable than merely mental prayer, which we will deal with later.

As for those others who benefit from the gift of prayer, hearing another pray is helpful to them in several respects. It shows them that the experiences of the one who prays are the same as their own. As sin works in one believer, so it works also in another. As grace works in one, so it also does in another. As he that prays longs for mercy and grace, so do they that join with him. Vocal prayer also directs those who hear to Scripture and shows its relevance and application to them.

Further, the one called to lead in prayer must pray for others out of a knowledge of their particular needs. He who is constantly to be the mouth of others to God is not to pray at random as though all persons and conditions were the same. He is to pray for others with particular watchfulness and observation. As a minister is obliged to consider the ways, light, knowledge and behaviour of his flock as he preaches to them, so he is no less bound to do this in his praying for them, if he intends that his prayers should be profitable to them.

According to James, we are to pray for one another (*James* 5:16). This can only be done if those to be prayed for communicate their needs and their state to the one who is to pray. If this duty were more attended to, the minds of many might receive great relief and comfort.

4. *Finally, we are to take heed that we do not have the gift of prayer in our minds without the grace of prayer in our hearts.* Those who are in this state are likely to be filled with spiritual pride, the usual result of unsanctified light.

We must also take care that we do not neglect to stir up the grace of prayer in our hearts and so come to depend merely on knowledge, imagination, memory and fluency of speech. He who watches his soul and all its activities will easily know when he has been sinfully negligent in this matter, or when he has paid more attention to the gift than to the grace of prayer, and will be humbled on this account.

We are now to give some attention to mental or contemplative prayer, as particularly favoured by some in the church of Rome, and in conclusion to prescribed forms of prayer.

10: Contemplative Prayer Considered

Having described the gift of prayer we must briefly examine what is sometimes set up in competition with it by devout persons in the church of Rome. This is *mental prayer*, which is said to be 'pure spiritual prayer, or a quiet repose of contemplation'.

It is said that to enter into such prayer requires 'an entire calmness and even death of the passions, a perfect purity in the spiritual affections of the will, and an entire abstraction from all creatures'.

OBJECTIONS TO CONTEMPLATIVE PRAYER

1. I cannot but approve of any attempt to have real spiritual intercourse of soul with God in prayer, but we must be careful not to delude ourselves. To lay down rules for prayer based on the reported experiences of others is dangerous to all who follow such instructions. The experiences which people claim to have had must be tested by Scripture. We must not be led astray by extravagant claims to wonderful experiences, especially when it is said that the mind or understanding must play no part in the activity of contemplation. Our worship is not to be irrational but rather our 'reasonable service'.

The descriptions of contemplative prayer appear to be borrowed from the contemplative philosophers of old who tried to refine heathenism and make it more acceptable to an increasingly Christian world. Plotinus (205–270 AD), for example, speaks in his *Enneads* of the mind being raised to perfect peace and calm, utterly undisturbed by feelings either of anger or of desire. Reason and understanding become passive. The soul is in an ecstasy and filled with God, and so enters into a quiet, still, immovable rest, a perfect state. All the contemplative philosophers of the time speak in this way.

2. I admit that in prayer our minds should be taken up with God in Christ until the soul is swallowed up in admiration and delight and loses itself in the infinity of those glorious excellencies which it adores. These are things to be aimed at in prayer, and through the riches of divine condescension they are frequently enjoyed.

However, this is not so much a matter of ecstasies or unaccountable raptures, as of that 'joy inexpressible and full of glory' spoken of by Peter. The soul is indeed helped in this contemplation by the Spirit of grace and the lively impressions of divine love, but at no time does the mind become inactive. That contemplative prayer advocated by some devout Roman Catholics has no support from Scripture. Its claim to bring the soul into perfect purity and the like cannot be confirmed by the rational experience of any, nor does it in any way remove the need for and usefulness of vocal prayer.

Our Lord Jesus Christ not only taught his disciples to pray by the use of words, but did so himself invariably, as far as we know (*Matt.* 26:39, 42). In fact when he was most intensely engaged in prayer, instead of this pretended contemplative prayer of quietness and stillness of mind, he prayed with 'vehement cries' (*Heb.* 5:7), and with 'the words of my groaning' (*Psa.* 22:1). All reproaches cast on earnest, vocal prayer, as tedious, loud, impetuous and an uncivilized way to converse with God, may with equal truth be cast on the way our Lord Jesus Christ prayed. Neither the apostles nor the prophets taught this mindless contemplative prayer, but constantly made use of and desired God to hear their 'voices', their 'cry', their 'words', in their prayers.

The use of words in prayer is very helpful in stirring up our innermost desires. This leads to words expressing those desires, which in turn stir up the mind and will to pray more fervently. The person who does not pray aloud often finds it more difficult to fight against distractions and diversions. And we have experience that an obedient, sanctified use of gracious words in prayer has prevailed against violent temptations of Satan which silent contemplation was not able to grapple with.

3. The dependence of this way of prayer on indescribable experiences casts doubt on its usefulness. It rouses up vain curiosity by which men 'intrude themselves into those things which they have not seen, being vainly puffed up by their own fleshly minds'. No-one can understand anything which he cannot experience. If I cannot have the same experience as you, then whatever you say about your experience to me is as meaningless as if you spoke to me in a foreign language which I do not understand. And if you say you came by that experience by feelings only, and that your mind was passive, how then can you explain that experience to yourself? All you can do is say, 'I have had an experience!' Or as one of the Roman contemplatives claimed, 'In my spiritual state, the essence of God touched me.' Such fanciful imaginations had better be kept to oneself than to be expressed in words bordering on blasphemy, or whose best defence is that the whole experience was wholly unintelligible. It is very dangerous in matters of religion to allow people to talk of experiences which they cannot understand themselves. This is a good way to introduce Babel into the church and expose the church to ridicule.

4. Contemplative prayer is altogether useless for the building up of the church. If Paul would not allow the use of words,

though miraculously suggested to those who used them, without an immediate interpretation giving their meaning, what would he have said of such experiences as none can interpret?

Will this encourage others to worship, that many in the church have wonderful experiences which they cannot understand and cannot explain to others? We may well ask, 'Of what good then are such wonderful experiences to us?' As no-one can understand the meaning of these experiences, they must therefore be the subject of everlasting wranglings and disputes. Who can assure us that those who claim such wonderful experiences are not frauds?

If a man claims to enjoy those things taught in God's Word which are for all believers and acknowledged by all to be true and real, his claim is to be believed unless he can be shown to be a hypocrite. Even if he deceives us, we know that what he claimed to enjoy is that which every believer should be enjoying for himself. But if any man claims to have had a wonderful experience which is not promised in Scripture and cannot be proved to be valid from Scripture, nor can it be examined in the light of reason, he is not to be taken seriously, and we are not obliged to believe him.

Once men allow themselves to be taken off from the sure foundation of Scripture and their own understanding, and cast on the uncertain waters of fanciful conjecture, they do not know how they may be tossed and where they may be driven to.

It is not lack of charity that makes us doubtful and unbelieving, but godly jealousy and Christian prudence. Claims to ecstasies, revelations and unaccountable enjoyments of God have been used for evil purposes. The experience of the church under both the Old Testament and the New witnesses to such false claims (*2 Pet.* 2:1). Under the Old Testament, there were those who 'wore a rough garment to deceive', and practised such austerities as gave them the appearance of great holiness and honesty. And when the body of the people grew corrupt and superstitious, these false prophets were more looked to than were the true prophets of God. Yet most of them were shown to be nothing but hypocrites. And we have warnings in the New Testament of those who will come into the church and lead many astray. So if we would not fall prey to deceivers we must try every spirit by the unerring rule of Scripture (*1 John* 4:1–2).

Those who claim to have had such experiences may be honestly persuaded in their own minds of the reality of them, but this will not give us assurance that what they tell us is true. Men may be so possessed with false ideas and imaginations that they think their delusions genuine and true. There are many ways by which men can be deceived, especially if they are superstitious and are encouraged by false teachings to expect such wonderful experiences. Since these acts of devotion require the mind to be passive, so that the whole act is irrational, it is not unreasonable for us to treat them as delusions.

That people can pray inwardly without giving voice to their prayers is admitted. But the mental or contemplative prayer contended for in which the mind is inactive is not prayer in the proper meaning of the word.

5. The common sense of mankind sees prayer as that acting of the mind and soul towards God in which we recognize our dependence on him and willingly come to him with all our concerns. The gospel shows us how to come to him through Christ with the aid of the Spirit of God, but does not introduce another idea of prayer contrary to this common notion. All the sailors who were on the ship with Jonah knew how to

call upon their gods when they were in a storm. But the contemplative prayer contended for involves no activity of faith, love, confidence or gratitude because the mind lies passive and inert. Those who advocate it had better find another name for it, for it has nothing to do with calling on God.

6. Finally, the contemplative prayer we are speaking of receives as little countenance from Scripture as it does from the light of nature. In Scripture prayer is the soul's access to God by Jesus Christ, through the help of the Spirit, to make known its requests, with supplication and thanksgiving. No-one can attend to this without the exercise of his mind and understanding.

In all the places where the nature and excellency of the duty and privilege of prayer are described (for example, *Eph.* 6:18; *Phil.* 4:6; *Heb.* 4:16; 10:19–22), there is nothing mentioned which is consistent with the notion of contemplative prayer. Nor is there anything in the example of our Lord Jesus Christ, his apostles, or any holy men from the beginning of the world, which gives the least countenance to it. Whatever is fancied or taught concerning it is utterly foreign to Scripture and must therefore arise from the deluded imagination of the few who advocate it.

Scripture allows no approach to God other than through the mediation of Jesus Christ and by faith in him. But the experience held out seems to promise a direct enjoyment of God in his essence regardless of Christ. God will not be all in all directly to the church until the Lord Christ has fully delivered up his mediatorial kingdom to him.

All the activities of our souls towards God must be a *reasonable service* (*Rom.* 12:1). Nothing more is required of us in a way of duty. But that in which our minds and understandings are not involved cannot be reasonable service. Nor can it be a means of our enjoying God in this life, since no such thing is promised to us anywhere in Scripture.

What is said for contemplative prayer seems to invent a kind of purgatory in devotion, above the attainments of this life, but very far short of future glory; out of this world, but not in another; above the earth, but beneath heaven. We will leave it there, in clouds and darkness.

11: Set Forms of Prayer
Examined

Prescribed forms of prayer are also pleaded for in opposition to that spiritual ability in prayer which we have shown to be a gift of the Holy Spirit. I am not concerned here with those who defend their own use of set forms, as serving God with the best that they have, but with the claim that these forms are *necessary*. This claim leads some to oppose and speak evil of the way of prayer which I have been describing. I would make the following observations:

1. *The Holy Spirit is nowhere promised to help any to compose prayers for others.* Therefore we have no warrant to pray for his help in this. The prayers of holy men recorded in Scripture, received by the direct inspiration of the Holy Spirit, are not a precedent in this matter. Men since do not have that inspiration, and it is doubtful if the prayers in Scripture were meant to be mere forms for others.

2. *No man has any promise that the Spirit of grace and supplication will enable him to compose a form or forms of prayer for himself.* The Spirit of God helps us to pray, not to compose prayers for use at any time we choose. When we pray the Spirit stirs up faith, love and delight in God within us. But when men compose prayers they are more concerned with the composition than with God directly. There is no promise of help from the Spirit in such compositions.

3. *The composition of such forms was not instituted under either law or gospel.* Therefore there will be no special help of the Spirit of God in it, as there would be if God had commanded such a

work to be done. I am not saying this to prove forms of prayer to be unlawful – only showing that they are not part of that work of the Spirit which I have been describing.

4. *It is doubtful if forms of prayer really benefit anyone.* What the alleged benefit is has not been clearly shown. If we have a spiritual ability and fail to use it, are we not neglecting to stir up the gift or grace of God that is within us? And what benefit is there in this?

As for those who find difficulty in praying for themselves, will not the use of prescribed forms of prayer tend to keep them in that state all their lives? Their ability will only be improved by constant exercise.

What if those spoken of are not real believers? If they have no spiritual light, set forms of prayer will be of little use to them. If they have some light and knowledge of the gospel, it is their duty to pray according to the light and knowledge that has been given to them.

5. *Arguments based on experience can be misleading.* Some claim that prescribed forms of prayer have helped them to have real spiritual fellowship with God. Must they not then be truly beneficial?

Here we must remember that there is a great difference between natural devotion and that spiritual devotion inspired by faith and love with other graces of the Spirit according to the mind and will of God. All who confess the existence of a deity or divine power which they worship and adore will have their feelings excited and roused by whatever means of worship they use, even if in reality their deity exists only in their imaginations. Some of the temples of the heathen are designed to create feelings of dread, reverence and fear in all who enter them, even though the gods worshipped there are only imaginary. Men are apt to be satisfied and delighted with the things they invent for themselves, as was Micah with his false gods (*Judg.* 17:13). Devotees of false gods satisfy their consciences by carrying out the duties imposed upon them even if those duties are meaningless and quite irrational.

But true gospel worship is of a different nature altogether. It is not stirred up by the inventions of men playing upon human nature but is the effect of the Holy Spirit working on renewed minds. Unless we know how to distinguish these things, it is to no purpose to say that some derive great spiritual help from prescribed forms of prayer. It is possible that the help they receive is no more than what all false worshippers in the world experience.

But it may also be that benefit *is* received because those who use set forms have prepared themselves beforehand by holy meditation and sincerely seek to worship God, so that they actually do exercise the grace they have received in the prayers they engage in.

Where people walk before God in integrity, and practise nothing contrary to their light and conscience in his worship, God is merciful to them, although everything is not regulated according to his Word.

Those who came to the passover in the days of King Hezekiah had not cleansed themselves, 'yet they ate the Passover contrary to what was written'. Hezekiah prayed for them: 'May the good LORD provide atonement for everyone who prepares his heart to seek God, the LORD God of his fathers, though he is not cleansed according to the purification of the sanctuary' (*2 Chron.* 30:18–19). 'And the LORD listened to Hezekiah and healed the people' (verse 20). God graciously passed by the people's offence and accepted them because their hearts were upright in what they did.

ARE SET FORMS OF PRAYER UNLAWFUL?

It will be asked at this point, Are such forms of prayer lawful or not? I would say:

1. *To compose forms of prayer as directive and doctrinal helps is lawful and may in some cases be useful.* It might be better to do this in another form, but this method of instruction is not to be considered unlawful just because of the form in which it is cast.

2. *To read, consider and meditate on written prayers so as to learn what to pray for and arguments to be used in prayer is lawful.* They are specially helpful if they have been written by godly persons from their own experience and in the light of Scripture. These prayers can be particularly useful where the hearts of those who read them are truly affected and helped to see their real state and condition.

3. *To set up and prescribe the use of set forms of prayer for everyone to the exclusion of free prayer by the aid of the Spirit is against many divine commands,* and also against the light of nature itself which requires every man to pray according to his own ability and in his own words.

4. *It is not suggested that prescribed forms of prayer are essentially evil.* It is granted that they are not. What we are considering is whether they do not hinder true prayer according to the mind of God, and so may be unlawful in that respect. Provided they are not used in such a way as to exclude the work of the Spirit in prayer which we have described from Scripture, or urged in such a way as to contravene a divine prohibition, I will not contend with anyone about them.

I will only give brief answers to some of the dubious arguments urged in their defence, and then conclude this discussion.

ARGUMENTS FOR SET FORMS

1. *Some say that forms of prayer were composed and prescribed for use in the Old Testament and the New.* They cite as examples the form of blessing prescribed for use by the priests (*Num.* 6:22–26), the Psalms of David and the Lord's Prayer in the New Testament.

If this were so, it would only prove that forms of prayer are not essentially evil, which is granted. But the argument will not stand. Even if God prescribed forms of prayer to be used by some persons on some occasions, it would not follow that men may invent prayers to be used by all on all occasions. He who forbade the use of images in sacred things appointed the making of the cherubim in the tabernacle and the temple. Also it would not be legitimate to argue from Old Testament practice to the duty and practice of believers under the New Testament, when the Spirit is much more abundantly poured out. The words prescribed to the priests were not properly a prayer, but an authoritative blessing. It was an instituted sign of God's blessing the people: 'They shall put my name on the children of Israel; and I will bless them.'

David's Psalms were given by direct inspiration and most of them were mystical and prophetical. They were appointed to be used in the church, as were all the other Scriptures. Some of them were to be sung, but this also was by divine appointment.

That any form of prayer is appointed in the New Testament to be used as a set form of prayer cannot be proved. Show me prayers composed by divine inspiration with a command and directions for their use and I will be satisfied with prescribed forms of prayer. All the examples of prayer given in Scripture were uttered in the freedom of men's own spirits. So they all testify to free prayer, if not against the use of set forms.

2. *When anyone prays in public his prayer becomes a set form to all that join with him.* The question is solely about the one praying and how he carries out the duty of prayer. We are not concerned with those who join with him. But that others should join with him in his prayer is the express command of God, and those who join with him are perfectly free, when it is their duty, to pray for themselves.

That which is not a set form in itself is not a set form to anyone else. More is required to make something a set form than that the words and expressions are not one's own. The one who is enabled by God's Spirit to lead in prayer is a gift of God to his people for their edification. Only what is used as a set form by someone is a set form to him. Its nature depends on its use.

Moreover this argument does not follow: 'God has commanded men to pray according to the ability they have received, and others to join with them in their prayers. Therefore it is lawful to invent forms of prayer for ourselves or others to be used as prayers by them or us.'

3. *Prayer itself is a commanded duty. But the way we pray, whether with prescribed forms or not, does not really matter.* It would be quite easy to prescribe such outward forms and ways of worship as to leave nothing but the shell of the duty, that is, the outward form of godliness, while denying the inward reality and power. Praying before an image, or worshipping God or Christ using an image, is only an outward form of worship, but it makes the whole thing idolatrous. Any outward form of worship which hinders the right performance of the duty concerned is not expedient. Whether this applies in the present case must be decided on the basis of the preceding discussion.

Part Four

The Holy Spirit as a Comforter

1: How the Spirit Comforts the Church

We are now to consider the office and work that the Holy Spirit has undertaken for the consolation of the church. We will note that he is the Comforter of the church as a special office and ask what the discharge of that office consists of, and what its effects are towards believers.

THE SPECIAL TRUST COMMITTED TO THE SPIRIT

Four things constitute an office: a special trust, a special mission or commission, a special name, and a special work.

The Spirit has been entrusted with this work and has willingly taken it on. The Lord Jesus Christ did not cease to care for his church when, having laid down his life for us, he returned to heaven (*Heb.* 4:14–16; 7:25–26). His care for the church on earth was entrusted to the Holy Spirit.

Christ's exaltation and return to heaven was necessary with respect to himself, for three reasons. Firstly, it was a pledge and token that God accepted him and approved of what he had done in the world (*John* 16:7–8; *1 Tim.* 3:16). Secondly his human nature, after all its labours and sufferings, deserved to be 'crowned with glory and honour' (*Luke* 24:26; *John* 17:4–5). Thirdly, it was necessary that he should take up the glorious administration of his kingdom from heaven (*Eph.* 1:21; *Phil.* 2:9–11).

The presence of the human nature of Christ in heaven was also necessary for our sakes (*Heb.* 7:25–27). It was necessary that he should 'appear in the presence of God for us' (*Heb.* 9:24).

As for the work especially entrusted to the Spirit, this consists in communicating spiritual light, grace and joy to believers, and it was no less the work of the Holy Spirit whilst the Lord Christ was on the earth than it is now when he is in heaven. But the full manifestation of this was reserved for the exaltation of Christ when he received the promise of the Spirit and poured it out on his disciples. Believers no longer look for grace and consolation directly from Christ in the flesh as the disciples did (*2 Cor.* 5:16).

The Lord Christ, though exalted, has not ceased to be the Comforter of the church. He is with us to the end of the world by his Spirit, and he dwells in us by his Spirit. Also, all the works of God towards us are works of Christ, as to his divine nature, and the Spirit, in his condescension, acts for Christ and in his name. Furthermore, all the light, grace and mercy by which the souls of Christ's disciples are comforted are the special fruits of Christ's mediation (*John* 16:14).

THE SPECIAL SENDING OF THE SPIRIT

The Spirit also has a special mission and commission given to him. One who is sent is entrusted with and empowered for the work he is sent to do (see *Psa.* 104:30; *John* 14:26; 15:26; 16:7). It is a great comfort, support and refreshment to believers to consider, not only that the Spirit is their Comforter, but that he is *sent* by the Father and the Son to be so. And there cannot be a greater evidence of the care of Christ for his people in all their sorrows and sufferings than this sending.

THE SPECIAL NAME GIVEN TO THE SPIRIT

The name of Paraclete *given to the Spirit denotes this special work.* It is applied to him by Christ in John's Gospel alone (*John* 14:16, 26; 15:26; 16:7). It is also applied to Christ (*1 John* 2:1–2), where we render it 'an Advocate'. The name may be best interpreted from the nature of the work assigned to the Spirit under that name. The main kind of work intended is that of a *Comforter*, as is clear from the context and occasion of Christ's promise of him. As Comforter, the Spirit brings a sense of love, with delight and joy, to the souls of believers (*Gal.* 5:22; *Rom.* 14:17; 5:5), filling us with 'joy unspeakable and full of glory'.

But the sense of *Advocate* is not to be neglected. He is not our advocate with God, for Christ alone is that. But he is an advocate for the church, in, with and against the world. In their defence of the truth of the gospel, and the power and kingdom of their Lord and Master, the disciples of Christ are helped and protected by the Spirit.

He does this, first, by suggesting to the witnesses of Christ appeals and arguments which will convince opposers of the gospel (*Matt.* 10:18-20; *Luke* 21:15; *Acts* 4:13). And he has continued in this defence of the cause of the gospel all through the history of the church. He does it, secondly, by giving spiritual gifts, both extraordinary and ordinary, to believers (*Gal.* 3:2). We will say more of these gifts in Part 4 of the present book. He does it, thirdly, in the preaching of the Word, by '*convincing* the world of sin, of righteousness and of judgment'(*John* 16:8–11). The Greek word used means to reprove or convince. It can also mean to 'reveal' or 'bring to light' (*Eph.* 5:13; *John* 3:20), or to 'rebuke' (*1 Tim.* 5:20; *Rev.* 3:19; *Tit.* 1:13). Sometimes it means so to convince that the mouth of an adversary is stopped, leaving him nothing to say by way of reply (*John* 8:9; *Tit.* 1:9, 11; see also *Heb.* 11:1).

The effect on the world is either that they surrender and receive the truth, finding no reason to reject it (*Acts* 2:41), or that they resist with desperate rage and madness (*John* 8:48, 59; 10:20, 31, 39; *Acts* 7:54–58; 22:22–23).

The subject-matter used by the Spirit as the Advocate of the church is 'sin, righteousness, and judgment'. He convinces the world of *sin* (*John* 16:9), especially the sin of not believing on the Lord Jesus Christ (*John* 8:21, 24). There are many sins of which men may be convinced by the light of nature (*Rom.* 2:14–15), and more that they are convinced of by the law. But the real cause that the Holy Spirit has to plead on the church's behalf against the world concerns the world's great sin of not believing in Jesus Christ. And in this work he continues till this day.

The second work of the Spirit on the world is to convince it of *righteousness*: 'Of righteousness, because I go to my Father and you see me no more.' Both Christ's personal righteousness, and the righteousness of his office are intended, for in both of these the church is in dispute with the world, and in them both the Holy Spirit is their Advocate. The world considered Christ an evil-doer, a seditious person, a seducer and a blasphemer. And as to the attaining of righteousness, the Gentiles looked to the light of nature and the Jews to the works of the law. The Spirit convinces the world that Christ has been exalted and taken up into glory, a proof of his righteousness and holiness (*Acts* 2:33). And in the preaching of the Word, the Spirit convinces those who hear of the impossibility of attaining to a righteousness of their own (*Rom.* 10:4).

The third work of the Spirit is to convince the world of *judgment*: 'Of judgment, because the ruler of this world is judged.' Christ was judged and condemned by the world. In that judgment, Satan, the ruler or prince of this world, had the chief hand. This judgment of Christ the world sought by all means to justify. But the Holy Spirit so defended Christ, in the cause of the church and through its faith, that the judgment was turned back on Satan himself. His lies about Christ were exposed and he was judged as an accursed apostate, a murderer and the great enemy of mankind. All the works of Satan, the superstition, idolatry and wickedness with which he had filled the world, were judged.

THE SPECIAL WORK COMMITTED TO THE SPIRIT

A special work is committed to the Spirit. This will appear more fully in the particulars that follow. At present I will only say in general that this work is to *support, cherish, relieve and comfort the church* in all her trials and distresses.

2: *The Characteristics of the Spirit's Work as Comforter*

The qualities or properties of this office and work of the Holy Spirit further illustrate its nature.

INFINITE CONDESCENSION

The condescension of the Holy Spirit in his work as a Comforter is beyond our understanding. It is different in its nature from that of the Son of God. The Spirit does not take our nature to himself as Christ did, nor expose himself to outward pains and sufferings. But that one Person in the Holy Trinity, existing in the unity of the same divine nature, should undertake to carry out the love and grace of the other Persons, in their names, is such a wonder as can only be fully understood by the Persons themselves. Our wisdom is simply to rest in what is revealed to us.

And the result of it is that he becomes a Comforter to us, poor, miserable worms of the earth. What heart can conceive the glory of this grace?

UNSPEAKABLE LOVE

The discharge of this office is accompanied by unspeakable love, working by tenderness and compassion. The Holy Spirit is said to be the divine, eternal, mutual love of the Father and the Son. Hence it is said that 'God is love' (*1 John* 4:8,16). That the Spirit, the eternal love of the Father and the Son, should choose this way of acting towards us is the most conspicuous example of his amazing love. For us to understand that it was infinite love which prompted the Spirit to take up this office of

Comforter has a great influence on our faith and obedience, and is the spring of all the consolations we receive from him. It is evident that it was so from the following considerations:

1. *From the nature of the work itself.* Giving comfort to another who stands in need of it is an immediate effect of love, especially when the one who comforts receives no advantage from doing so. We must believe that this work of the Spirit of God proceeds solely from his love if we are to receive any solid and lasting benefit from it.

2. *From the way in which the Spirit carries out this work.* 'As one whom his mother comforts, so I will comfort you; and you shall be comforted in Jerusalem' (*Isa.* 66:13). In natural terms, no better conception of love, care and tenderness can be formed than that of a tender mother who comforts her children in distress. And this is how the Holy Spirit comforts us. Just as a child may be ungrateful to its mother out of the bitterness of its pain and distress, so a believer may for a time show no gratitude for divine comforts, but the great Comforter knows how to bear with and overcome these things. God, by his Spirit, will 'revive the spirit of the humble, and . . . the heart of the contrite ones' (*Isa.* 57:15), even if he has to use sharp remedies for their spiritual recovery. Only infinite love and compassion, working by patience and longsuffering, could lift us out of our distresses.

3. *From the fact that we are cautioned not to grieve the Spirit (Eph. 4:30).* Others may be vexed or angered, but only those who love us can be grieved by us. We see his love in that he undertakes to comfort those who are so apt and prone to grieve him, as we generally are. He commends his love to us in that he recovers us from those ways of ours which are such a grief to him.

INFINITE POWER

Also evident in this work of the Holy Spirit as Comforter is his infinite power. The church complains, 'My way is hidden from the LORD, and my just claim is passed over by my God' (*Isa.* 40:27). It is not so much her sorrows and troubles that the church complains of, as the feeling of being ignored by God. How then does God comfort the church? He answers her, 'Have you not known? Have you not heard? The everlasting God, the LORD, the Creator of the ends of the earth, neither faints nor is weary. His understanding is unsearchable' (verses 28–31).

The church seems to doubt, not his power, but his love, care and faithfulness to her. But it is his infinite power that he chooses first to reassure her of, then his infinite understanding and wisdom. We should first grasp his infinite power, then leave everything to his sovereign wisdom and understanding. The church's complaint arose from disbelief of his infinite power and wisdom. So, in the work of the Holy Spirit as Comforter, we must especially consider his infinite power. The apostle John proposes this for the support of the weakest believer, 'He who is in you is greater than he who is in the world' (*1 John* 4:4). The Holy Spirit who dwells in us is infinitely greater than Satan, the world, and all their opposition.

Faith in his infinite power is needed for any solid spiritual comfort. Dejected believers will sometimes reject all comfort not brought with almighty efficacy. Therefore God creates 'the fruit of the lips, Peace, peace' (*Isa.* 57:19), producing peace in the souls of men by a creating act of his power. Only the almighty Spirit of God can be the church's Comforter. The peace and comfort of believers are threatened by the power of hell, of sin and of the world, but God declares that it is he who comforts his people: 'I, even I, am he who comforts you. Who are you that you should be afraid of a man who will die, and of the son of a man who will be made like grass? And you forget the LORD your Maker, who stretched out the heavens and laid the foundations of the earth; you have feared continually every day because of the fury of the oppressor, when he has prepared to destroy. And where is the fury of the oppressor?' (*Isa.* 51:12–13).

Therefore when we are fearful and discouraged, and see the church so weak and our enemies so strong, let us remember that our Comforter is of almighty power, wonderful in counsel, and excellent in working.

UNCHANGEABLE CONSTANCY

This work of the Holy Spirit as Comforter is unchangeable. He abides for ever as a Comforter with all those to whom he is given. This our Saviour declared in the first promise he made of sending him as a Comforter: 'I will pray the Father, and he will give you another Comforter, that he may abide with you forever' (*John* 14:16). Our Saviour was preparing the hearts of his disciples for his departure from them. They might imagine that this other Comforter, the Holy Spirit, would also depart from them after a time. To assure their minds on this matter, the Lord Jesus Christ lets them know that this other Comforter would not only always be with them to the end of their lives, work and ministry, but that he would abide with the church absolutely until the consummation of all things. The Spirit is now given to the church in an eternal and unchangeable covenant (*Isa.* 59:21).

It might be objected that, if the Comforter abides always with the church, it is strange that so many believers spend perhaps the greatest part of their lives in troubles and sorrows with no experience of the presence of the Holy Spirit with them as a Comforter. But this objection should not weaken our faith in the accomplishment of the promise, for:

1. The very promise of a Comforter to abide with the church forever shows that believers in all ages were to meet with trouble, sorrow and distress.

2. Our feelings in our troubles can mislead us as to the fulfilment of the promise, especially when a measure of unbelief is present. The church thinks herself forsaken by God (*Isa.* 40:27; 49:14). But God convinces her that she is mistaken and that her complaint is the result of her unbelief. So believers, swallowed up with sorrow, are often not aware of the work of the Holy Spirit in comforting them.

3. The Holy Spirit is a Comforter to believers at all times and in all situations in which they really need his comfort. But we can, through neglect, fail to enjoy the comforts he is willing to give. We must understand aright the nature of spiritual comforts, and value them, if we are to enjoy them. We must not suppose that there is no comfort until our particular troubles are removed, or value outward relief above inward support and refreshment. If we are found in fervent prayer for the Spirit's presence and the manifestation of his grace, in holy obedience and dependence on him, we shall certainly find him a Comforter to us.

3: The Holy Spirit Comforts Only Believers

Our enquiry in this chapter is, to whom is the Holy Spirit promised as a Comforter? Who receive him as such? He is promised as a Comforter to all believers in Christ, and to no others (*John* 14:16–17, 26; 15:26; 16:7– 8).

The promise was first given to the apostles, but not because they were apostles; rather because they were believers and disciples of Christ, and because of the fierce opposition they would meet with from the world.

Christ also taught that the Holy Spirit could not be received by the world (*John* 14:17). The Spirit does indeed act on the world, for their conviction and the conversion of many of them, but as a Spirit of consolation he cannot be received by them until other gracious acts of his have taken place in them. All his acts as Comforter presuppose saving faith.

Receiving the Holy Spirit as Comforter is the great fundamental privilege of true believers, by which, through the grace of our Lord Jesus Christ, they are exalted above all other persons in this world.

All the wisest men in all ages have acknowledged the truth that the life of man is subject to innumerable troubles (*Job* 5:7). But what comfort has all their philosophy been able to offer? All it has amounted to is this, that the true exercise of reason shows that what we think evil or grievous is not really so. But what consolation is this, compared with the privilege of believers in the provision made for them in the One in whom they believe? In this matter the Sun of Righteousness (*Mal.* 4:2) has risen and shines on all who live in the land of Goshen, while those who remain in Egypt have only lanterns to see by (*Exod.* 10:23). And if believers rightly considered what an advantage they have in this, through the love and care of Jesus Christ, they would rejoice in it more than in all that the world can give.

This, then, is not the first saving work of the Holy Spirit on the souls of men. Regeneration and sanctification always precede it. The Spirit comforts none but those whom he has first sanctified. No others can benefit from his work as Comforter, for they are incapable of appreciating it. This is why the whole work of the Holy Spirit as Comforter, the fulfilment of the most glorious promise that Christ ever made to his church, is so neglected and despised by so many professing Christians. It is an evidence of the fallen state of the Christian profession. If men are not first sanctified by the Holy Spirit, they can never be comforted by him.

What remain to be considered are the particular acts of the Spirit which belong to his work as Comforter and the privileges which believers receive by them. We will do this briefly in the chapters which follow.

4: The Indwelling of the Holy Spirit

The first thing promised to believers concerning the Holy Spirit as Comforter is that he should dwell in them. All other privileges depend on this.

The indwelling of the Spirit in believers is one of those things which must be firmly believed, even though we may not fully understand it.

DISTINCT FROM OMNIPRESENCE

The presence of the Holy Spirit everywhere and in all things is not the same thing as his personal indwelling in believers. As God, one and the same in being and substance with the Father and the Son, he fills all things and is everywhere present, but his indwelling is personal, belongs distinctly to him as the Spirit of God, and is voluntary. It wholly depends on a free act of his will.

DISTINCT FROM THE SPIRIT'S GRACIOUS WORK

The promise of the Spirit's indwelling is not just that he will work graciously in us. This he could do without dwelling in us. He is essentially everywhere and can work where and how he pleases without indwelling any person. What is promised to believers is the Spirit himself and his coming to live in them in a special way: 'He will be in you.'

DISTINCT FROM A PERSONAL UNION

There is no *personal union* between the Holy Spirit and the believer. What we call a personal union is the union of different natures in the same person, making only one person. The union of Christ's human and divine natures in one Person is such a personal union. Christ is not two persons, but one Person with two perfect natures, the divine and the human.

So the indwelling of the Holy Spirit in believers does not bring about a personal union between the Holy Spirit and the believer, for each is a distinct person, and must eternally be so whilst their natures are distinct from each other.

BRINGS ABOUT UNION WITH CHRIST

Indwelling brings about union with Jesus Christ. What is brought about is the union of believers with Christ *by* the Spirit, not union *with* the Spirit himself. The Spirit is sent by Christ to dwell in believers, in his name, as his Spirit. Hence arises a mystical union between Christ and believers, of which the Spirit is the bond and vital principle.

Considering this, I say that it is the person of the Holy Spirit that is promised to believers and not only the effects of his grace and power. As well as showing his infinite condescension, this is one great proof of his eternal deity, since one and the same Person can at the same time indwell so many thousands of distinct persons. Therefore what some think beneath his glory is a wonderful demonstration of his glory. Only an infinite being can be *with* and *in* all believers in the world. And none but he who is infinite can personally indwell all believers equally. While we cannot understand this, we are humbly to believe and receive it as truth.

PROMISED IN THE OLD TESTAMENT

There are many promises in the Old Testament that God would give the Holy Spirit, under the terms of the new covenant (*Ezek.* 36:27; *Isa.* 59:21; *Prov.* 1:23).

God always calls this promised Spirit, 'My Spirit', denoting the Person of the Spirit himself. Some understand by these promises only the gracious works of the Holy Spirit, and not his personal indwelling. But these promises as expounded in the New Testament are not limited to his gracious works alone. They also relate to his Person, as indwelling believers.

GIVEN IN ANSWER TO PRAYER

We are taught to pray for the Holy Spirit, and are assured that God will give him to those who ask (*Luke* 11:13). If what we ask for is not the Holy Spirit personally, but only his works of grace and power, it must follow that asking for his personal indwelling does not agree with other testimonies of Scripture, or is absurd and unreasonable, or is contrary to the experience of believers. None of these is true. There are many Scriptures which testify to the personal indwelling of the Spirit in believers. David prayed that God would not take his Holy Spirit from him (*Psa.* 51:11). Believers in Scripture pray that God would give his Spirit to them. Even after having received the Holy Spirit we should continually pray such prayers. Do believers pray only for the outward gracious works of the Holy Spirit? Will thoughts of grace and mercy satisfy them once they learn that the Holy Spirit does not live in them? They may not understand how the Spirit can live in them, yet it is for him personally that they pray. Without the assurance of his indwelling presence with them they can have neither peace nor comfort.

PROMISED DISTINCTLY BY CHRIST

Christ distinctly points his disciples to the indwelling of the Holy Spirit (*John* 14:17). Other Scriptures also speak clearly of this blessing (*Rom.* 8:9, 11. See also *2 Tim.* 1:14; *1 John* 4:4).

THE SPRING OF THE SPIRIT'S WORKS IN US

All the gracious works of the Holy Spirit in us and towards us as the Comforter depend on his indwelling us. He is that 'fountain of water' in us 'springing up into everlasting life' (*John* 4:14). The water here promised by Christ is the Holy Spirit, called the 'gift of God' (*John* 4:10; see also *John* 7:38–39). This 'fountain of water' is to be in us and abide in us, which is a figurative way of describing the indwelling of the Holy Spirit. This cannot refer only to a gracious work of the Holy Spirit in us. Nor can any quality he produces in our minds be a fountain of living water. The Holy Spirit in his indwelling is distinct from all his evangelical works of grace as the fountain is distinct from the water flowing from it. And as it is natural and easy for a fountain of water to bubble up and pour out refreshing streams so the comfort of believers lies in knowing how ready the Holy Spirit is to carry on his works of grace, holiness and sanctification in us until he has perfected them. Other Scriptures show the indwelling of the Spirit to be the cause or fountain of all his gracious activities in us (*Rom.* 5:5; 8:11, 16).

This indwelling is the secret reason for the wonderful and inexpressible difference between believers and the rest of the world. Their 'life is hid with Christ in God' (*Col.* 3:3). This life which believers have in them cannot be seen by the world because it is 'hidden'. By it believers are set apart from the world which is perishing. The difference concerned is real and great. Those who believe enjoy the special love and favour of God, while those who do not believe do not have this 'life' in them, are 'under the curse', and 'the wrath of God abides on them'. If men will not believe that there is this great difference between believers and unbelievers in this world, they will be forced to admit it at the last day, when they hear it said to believers, 'Come, you blessed', and to unbelievers, 'Go, you

[158]

cursed'. As far as the world is concerned, there is no difference between themselves and believers. So the world misjudges believers, both as to what they are and as to what they do.

There is a great difference between the works of believers and those of unbelievers, and this difference ought to be far greater than it is. If there were a greater difference here, a greater testimony would be given to the righteousness of God (*1 John* 3:12).

There is a still greater difference between believers and unbelievers in that internal grace by which the minds of believers are transformed into the image of God (*Tit.* 1:15).

But the chief difference between them lies in the indwelling of the Holy Spirit. The great difference between the two houses that Solomon built was that God dwelt in one and Solomon in the other. Two houses may look similar from the outside, but if the King lives in one and a robber in the other, the one is a Palace and the other a den. On this difference depend all the advantages which believers have above the men of the world, and it is a sufficient reason for all the excellent things which are spoken of those who are partakers of it.

5: *The Holy Spirit as an Anointing*

The first privilege that believers receive from the Holy Spirit as a Comforter which I shall speak of is the *unction* or *anointing* which they have from him: 'But you have an anointing from the Holy One' (*1 John* 2:20). This anointing is said to 'abide' in believers and to 'teach them concerning all things' (verse 27). We must first remove some misconceptions concerning what the anointing is.

NOT THE DOCTRINE OF THE GOSPEL

The anointing is not *the doctrine of the gospel*, or *the truth itself*. Neither the text nor the context will allow this interpretation for the following reasons:

The doctrine of the gospel was the matter in question. The false teachers claimed to have the true gospel, while the apostle denied their claim. But what he insists on for the help and comfort of believers is not the doctrine itself but the advantage they enjoyed for the right understanding of it, the anointing they had received.

Secondly, the anointing is said to abide in those who had received it, whereas we are said to abide in the doctrine we have received.

Thirdly, the anointing is said to teach us, whereas the gospel is what we are taught.

Fourthly, everywhere else in Scripture 'anointing' means either the Holy Spirit or some special work of his. There is no good reason why some other meaning should be imposed on the word as it is used here.

NOT THE SPIRIT'S WITNESS TO THE TRUTH

The anointing is not the testimony given to the truth by the Holy Spirit, that is, the miraculous gifts of the Spirit accompanying the first preaching of the gospel. All believers are anointed by God (*2 Cor.* 1:21), but not all believers had miraculous gifts. To have an anointing from the Holy One, an anointing which abides in us and teaches us, is clearly not the same thing as to have heard of the miraculous works of the Spirit vindicating the gospel and giving testimony to the truth.

NOT OUTWARD ANOINTING WITH OIL

The anointing is clearly not an anointing with oil, as some Roman Catholics teach. The more sober expositors among them admit this, in commenting on this passage.

THE TRUE MEANING OF THE ANOINTING

1. *Figurative anointings*: In the Old Testament, all persons and things dedicated to God, including kings, priests and prophets, were anointed with oil. All these pointed to Christ, in whom their purpose was fulfilled. So Christ was anointed as the Most Holy (*Dan.*9:24). The terms 'Messiah' under the Old Testament and 'Christ' under the New mean 'the Anointed One'.

2. *The anointing as applied to Christ*: How Christ was to be anointed is declared by Isaiah (*Isa.* 61:1). 'The Spirit of the Lord God is upon me, because the Lord has anointed me.' Christ's anointing consisted mainly in the giving of the Spirit to him. We can take it as a general rule that the anointing with material oil under the Old Testament symbolized the pouring out of the Holy Spirit under the New Testament. So the gospel is called the 'ministration of the Spirit' (*2 Cor.* 3:6, 8). The anointing of Christ was expressed in this way: 'The

Spirit of the LORD shall rest upon him, the Spirit of wisdom and understanding, the Spirit of counsel and might, the Spirit of knowledge and of the fear of the LORD' (*Isa.* 11:2).

Christ was anointed with the Holy Spirit in full measure to equip him with all the gifts and graces needed by his human nature or for his work. This anointing was carried out in different ways, at different times. He was anointed by the Spirit in his incarnation in the womb (*Luke* 1:35). He was anointed by the Spirit at his baptism (*Matt.* 3:16; *Isa.* 61:1). He was anointed by the Spirit for his death and sacrifice, for which he sanctified himself (*John* 17:19). And he was anointed by the Spirit at his ascension (*Acts* 2:33; see also *Heb.* 1:8–9).

3. *The anointing as applied to believers*: Believers have their anointing directly from Christ, called there 'the Holy One' (*1 John* 2:20); this title is applied to him elsewhere (*Acts* 3:14; *Rev.* 3:7; see also *Dan.* 9:24). The anointing is clearly the Holy Spirit which all believers receive (*Eph.* 3:16; *Phil.* 1:19). Believers are anointed by God (*2 Cor.* 1:21), by which we may understand that the Father is the original, supreme cause of our anointing, while Christ is the immediate, efficient cause of it. The anointing of believers therefore consists in the giving of the Holy Spirit to them, from and by Jesus Christ, and the One who anoints is not the Holy Spirit, but Christ.

This anointing, that is, the Holy Spirit, conveys spiritual teaching by illuminating the minds of believers to understand the mind of God and the mysteries of the gospel. By it believers know the truth and adhere firmly to it in love and obedience. And by it believers are specially dedicated to God and made 'kings and priests' (*Rev.* 1:6; *1 Pet.* 2:9), or a royal priesthood.

THE BENEFITS OF THE ANOINTING

The anointing establishes believers in the faith (1 John 2:20, 27). It keeps them from being carried away from the faith by the craft of seducers. The teaching concerned is not merely external doctrinal instruction, but an inward, effectual work of the Spirit (*Eph.* 1:17, 18), though it does make use of the outward means of instruction, and teaches nothing but what is revealed there. The Spirit opens our eyes, that we may clearly and spiritually see the wonderful things that are in the Word of God.

The anointing teaches believers all things necessary for their full salvation (1 John 2:20; John 14:26; 16:13). It teaches them in such a way as to bring them to love and thoroughly approve of the things which it teaches. It makes these things sweeter to us than honey or the honeycomb, quickening our minds to holy obedience, sanctifying and securing our souls to the end.

The anointing brings satisfaction, refreshment and joy to the soul in the clear apprehension of saving truth. This is part of the work of the Spirit as the church's Comforter. Most believers are often at a loss as to clearly apprehending their own spiritual state, confused as to their experiences, or misled by temptations, so that they do not receive a refreshing sense of the comforts and joys which really belong inseparably to the anointing. Nevertheless, the anointing remains the spring from which secret refreshment and support are ministered to them. And if they saw more clearly into the mysteries of the will, love and grace of God in Christ, as they should, they would have more of the consolation of knowing their acceptance with God, as being made kings and priests to him, and have a refreshment which the world knows nothing of.

6: The Holy Spirit Seals
    Believers

Another work of the Holy Spirit as Comforter of the church is that by him believers are sealed (*2 Cor.* 1:21–22; *Eph.* 1:13; 4:30). To say that believers are *sealed with the Spirit* implies that the Spirit is himself the seal, rather than that any of his special operations are. Sealing, then, appears to be a particular effect of the Spirit being given to us.

THE COMMON EXPLANATION OF SEALING

Sealing with the Spirit is commonly explained in terms of sealing with a wax seal among men. It is taken to mean the impressing of the Spirit's own nature and likeness on the souls of believers, so that it is substantially the same as sanctification.

Sealing is used among men for the security of deeds, grants, promises and wills. Believers may then be said to be sealed when the promises of God are confirmed to our souls and we are assured of them by the Spirit. But, in fact, this is to seal the promises of God and not believers, whereas it is persons, not promises, that are said to be sealed in Scripture.

Sealing is also used by men to keep safe what is sealed. Job speaks of his transgression being sealed up in a bag (*Job* 14:17). So believers are said to be sealed for safe-keeping by the Holy Spirit.

But on further consideration I am not satisfied that this is the exact meaning of the term in Scripture. There are so many uses of sealing among men that it is hard to determine what is meant when the word is applied to the Spirit. Moreover, all the usual explanations of sealing concern acts or effects of the

Spirit on us, whereas it is not said that *the Spirit seals us*, but that *we are sealed with him.* He is God's seal to us (*2 Cor.* 1:22).

WHAT IS SEALING WITH THE SPIRIT?

Because Christ is said to be sealed by God the Father (*John* 6:27), it will help us to understand the nature of this privilege if we can see the nature of sealing in his case. All our spiritual privileges consist in our sharing in the fountain-head and fulness of them in Christ. Just as we learn what anointing means from Christ's anointing, so we may learn what sealing means from Christ's sealing.

1. *What Christ's sealing is not*: The seal does not concern Christ's divine nature, for the communication of all the essential properties of the divine nature to him from the Father is by eternal generation, not by sealing.

Nor does it relate specifically to his kingly office, as some think, because what he directs the people to in John 6 is the spiritual nourishment they might receive from his Person, mediation and grace, not the benefits of his kingship particularly (see *John* 6:26–27).

2. *Why Christ was sealed*: The context in John 6 shows that Christ's sealing related to the dispensing of spiritual food to the souls of men. He was able to give his flesh to feed the souls of men because he had been sealed by the Father for this very purpose. The sealing also provided evidence that he was appointed by God to do so. Since it was God's seal, it testified of God's approval of him. By sealing Christ, the Father acknowledged him to be his Son, the One that he had sent into the world to nourish and feed men's souls (*John* 6:27; see also *Matt.* 3:17; 17.5; *2 Pet.* 1:17–18).

By this sealing God also showed that he would take care of Christ and keep him safe in his work until it was finished (see *Isa.* 42:1–4).

The sealing of the Son, then, is the giving of the Holy Spirit to him in all his fulness, authorizing and enabling him to carry out all the works and duties of his office in such a way as to prove clearly that God was with him. God cannot give a greater testimony of his approval of a person than the great seal of his Spirit, and this was given to Christ in all its fulness. He was 'declared to be the Son of God with power according to the Spirit of holiness' (*Rom.* 1:4) and 'justified in the Spirit' (*1 Tim.* 3:16). And this is undoubtedly our best guide to how Christ's members are sealed, since we all have our measure of the Spirit out of his fulness.

3. *How believers are sealed*: God's sealing of believers with the Holy Spirit is his gracious gift of the Holy Spirit to them, enabling them to fulfil all the duties of their holy calling, showing their acceptance with God both to themselves and to others, and attesting their preservation to eternal salvation. The effects of the sealing are the gracious works of the Holy Spirit in them and upon them, but the sealing itself is the communication of the Spirit to them. They are *sealed with the Spirit*.

When persons are called to become true believers they are brought into many new relationships: 'All things have become new' (*2 Cor.* 5:17). In this new world into which they are brought, how will they know how to behave, and how will they live up to the holy station in which they are placed?

To make this possible, God owns them as his and gives them his Spirit to fit them for their new position and relationships, so that they can carry out the work they are called to, just as their Head, the Lord Jesus Christ, did. God does not give them 'the spirit of fear, but of power and of love and of a sound mind' (*2 Tim.* 1:7). And in this way God seals them, for:

i. *By this sealing God bears witness to believers that they are his, accepted by him as his children.* God 'acknowledged [the Gentile believers] by giving them the Holy Spirit' (*Acts* 15:8–9).

ii. *By this sealing God gives to believers the assurance of their relationship to him and of his love and favour to them.* This is not by any particular work of the Holy Spirit in them, but the communication of the Spirit himself. 'By this we know that he abides in us, by the Spirit whom he has given us' (*1 John* 3:24; see also *Rom.* 8:9).

iii. *By this sealing God marks believers as his own.* The spiritual change in them will be noticed by the world, according to their own measure. It will be seen in the gifts and graces communicated to them, and will draw down on them the hatred which always exists on the part of the seed of Cain against the seed of Abel. And it follows from this that those who are sealed with the Spirit of God cannot but separate themselves from most of the world, which shows even more to whom they belong.

iv. *By this sealing God keeps believers safe till the day of redemption and eternal salvation.* The Spirit given to them is to abide with them for ever, as a fountain of water springing up to eternal life (*John* 4:14; 7:38).

This, then, is the seal which God grants to believers, that is, his Holy Spirit. And this, according to their measure, answers to the great seal of heaven which God gave to his Son in all its divine fulness, authorizing and enabling him for all the work he was called to do.

7: *The Holy Spirit as an Earnest or Guarantee*

W e have spoken of the Spirit as an anointing and as a seal. The third way in which he is spoken of which we will consider is as an *earnest, a guarantee, or a down-payment* (*2 Cor.* 1:22; 5:5; *Eph.* 1:14). In the New Testament original, the word concerned is used only of this matter.

THE SPIRIT HIMSELF IS THE EARNEST

It is the Holy Spirit himself, rather than any work of his on us or in us, who is the earnest or guarantee. The giving of the earnest is said to be the act of God the Father who, as Christ had promised, sent the Comforter to the church. This act of God is described as giving or putting him into our hearts (*2 Cor.* 1:22). He is given to dwell in us and to abide with us as an earnest of our future inheritance (*Eph.* 1:14).

There are aspects of earnests or pledges as used in human affairs which do not apply in this matter. All that is intended is the general purpose of an earnest: to give a guarantee of something yet to come. By this earnest God intends to assure us that he will give us much more in the future, at a time which he has appointed.

'THE GUARANTEE OF OUR INHERITANCE'

We receive the Spirit as the Spirit of Christ and from him. God has sent the Spirit of his Son into our hearts (*Gal.* 4:6) to make us partakers of his graces and privileges. Christ is the 'heir of all things' (*Heb.* 1:2). Man, by sin, lost his inheritance and forfeited all rights to earth and heaven. But God has in-vested the whole inheritance in his Son, making him the heir of it all. Now Christ, by his death, has redeemed the inheritance and purchased the possession of it for us. Hence it is called 'the purchased possession' (*Eph.* 1:14). Christ is now the great trustee for his people. He holds our inheritance in trust until that day when we shall enter into it. And all our interest in this inheritance depends on our union with him.

This in turn comes about through our partaking in the Spirit of Christ, as the apostle declares (*Rom.* 8:14–17). If we are children, we are heirs, and joint-heirs with Christ. The whole inheritance was his by right, but he has purchased a joint right to it for us.

But in the meantime, before we enter fully into it, we have an earnest or guarantee that we shall have it. We enter our inheritance fully only when our bodies are redeemed fully from the dust of the grave (*Rom.* 8:23). We have 'the firstfruits of the Spirit' and he gives us a foretaste of the glories to come. The inheritance itself I believe to be the highest participation with Christ in his glory and honour as 'heir of all things' that our natures are capable of receiving.

CONCLUSION

All evangelical privileges which believers have in this world centre in the Holy Spirit. He is the great promise that Christ made to his disciples, the great legacy that he has bequeathed to them. In this great privilege of receiving the Spirit, all others are wrapped up.

No one comparison can express the greatness of this privilege. It is *anointing*, it is *sealing*, it is *an earnest* and *a first-fruit* – everything by which the love of God and the blessed security of our state can be expressed, for what greater pledge can we have of the love and everlasting favour of God than that he has given us his Holy Spirit?

APPLICATION OF THIS DISCOURSE

How can we best comply with the Spirit in his work of grace towards us? There are things we must avoid, and things we must do. As to the first: 'Do not grieve the Holy Spirit of God, by whom you were sealed for the day of redemption' (*Eph.* 4:30). Remembering who he is and what he has done for us, how great our concern should be that he abides with us and never leaves us.

Our grieving him involves unkindness and ingratitude on our part, and disappointment, or what corresponds to this in an omniscient Being, on his. We grieve him when we are not influenced by his love and kindness so as to yield holy obedience, in joy, love and delight, to him; when we lose and forget the impression of the great mercies we receive from him; or when we fall into those sins which especially grieve him (*1 Cor.* 6:15-20; *Eph.* 4:29–30).

Even more should we beware of going further and vexing him (*Isa.* 63:10), which seems to be a heightening and aggravation of grieving him, perhaps by obstinate persistence in the things which cause him grief. The ultimate stage of this would be that he would become our enemy and fight against us, removing our gifts and graces and casting us out of his kingdom. After his sin, David dreaded that God might take his Holy Spirit from him (*Psa.* 51:11), and the awfulness of this thought should move us to the utmost care and diligence against sin. If we have grieved him by our negligence concerning our duties, by indulging any lust, by yielding to or conforming to the world, let us remember that he has all the necessary means to use for our healing and recovery. Let us diligently and speedily return to him, lest we provoke him to become our enemy.

Part Five

The Gifts of
the Holy Spirit

1: The Purpose of Spiritual Gifts

By his work of saving grace the Spirit makes all the elect *living stones*, and by his imparting of spiritual gifts he builds these stones into *a temple for the living God* to dwell in, spiritually uniting them into one mystical body under the headship of the Lord Jesus Christ. The members of this body have the same nature, by grace, but different uses, by the imparting of spiritual gifts. The gifts are not themselves saving graces, but they are not to be despised, because they are 'the powers of the age to come' (*Heb.* 6:5), by means of which the kingdom of Christ is preserved and propagated in the world. The things we are to inquire into are the *names* of these gifts, their *nature* (and how they differ from saving graces), the *distinctions* among them, and their *use* in the church of God.

THE NAMES OF SPIRITUAL GIFTS

The general name of these spiritual endowments is *gifts* (*Eph.* 4:8; see also *Psa.* 68:18). They are the free and undeserved effects of divine bounty, also called *charismata*, or gifts of generous grace (*Rom.* 12:6; *1 Cor.* 1:7; 7:7; 12:4, 9, 28, 30; *2 Tim.* 1:6; *1 Pet.* 4:10). As to their especial nature, they are *spiritual gifts* (*1 Cor.* 12:1; 14:1, 31). They are not natural or moral endowments but spiritual endowments. Their author is the Holy

Spirit; their nature is spiritual; and the things they have to do with are spiritual things.

HOW SPIRITUAL GIFTS ARE COMMUNICATED

As to the manner of their communication these gifts are called 'distributions of the Holy Spirit' (*Heb*. 2:4). They are called this because the Spirit, the author of them, distributes them as he sees fit, variously, as the edification of the church requires. Their variety both beautifies and benefits the church, and their varied distribution makes it a true body. If there were only one gift, or gifts of only one kind, the whole body would be only one member, and if there were none the body would not be animated at all, but a dead carcase.

The diversity of the gifts is described by the apostle in 1 Corinthians 12:8–10. Although the edification of the church is the general objective of them all, this requires various distinct and different gifts.

Again, the nature of the operations they enable those who receive them to perform is reflected in the terms used of them, particularly *ministrations, or ministries* (*1 Cor*. 12:5) and *activities, or operations* (*1 Cor*. 12:6). They are all comprised in the apostle's expression 'the manifestation of the Spirit' (*1 Cor*. 12:7), since in and by them all the Spirit manifests his power.

2: Spiritual Gifts and Saving Grace

The nature of spiritual gifts and the difference between these and saving grace are the next things to be considered.

SPIRITUAL GIFTS AND SAVING GRACE: SIMILARITIES

1. *Both spiritual gifts and saving grace are purchased by Christ for his church and are the fruits of his mediation.*

The gifts we are speaking of are those which belong to the kingdom set up by the Lord Jesus Christ after his ascension into heaven. The power of communicating these gifts was granted by the Father to Christ as Mediator for the foundation and edification of his church (*Acts* 2:33). They were the weapons of warfare given to his disciples to subdue the world to the obedience of the gospel and to overthrow the kingdom of Satan and of darkness in the world (*Acts* 1:4, 8; *2 Cor.* 10:3–6).

Through the neglect of these gifts in the matters of praying, preaching, interpretation of the Scriptures, and the administration and worship of the church, an apostasy came in which allowed Satan to set up his kingdom again, though not in the old way. Instead of the old paganism and heathenism he set up a papal antichristian system which professed conformity with the letter of the Word of God, but finally came to be completely contrary to it.

By these gifts the Lord Christ showed his power and exercised his rule. External force and carnal weapons were far from his thoughts, nor were they needed.

2. *Both spiritual gifts and saving grace are wrought by the power of the Holy Spirit.*

I have already shown that saving grace comes by the power of the Spirit. That spiritual gifts also come by his power is declared every time they are mentioned in Scripture. And, in fact, this is denied only by those who deny that any such gifts continue in the church.

3. *Both spiritual gifts and saving grace are for the good, beauty and glory of the church.*

The church is the proper place for the display of both, for Christ loved the church and gave himself for her to sanctify and cleanse her (*Eph.* 5:26–27). This is the work of saving grace, by which alone men become members of this true, believing church. But gifts are bestowed on the professing church to make the working of saving grace visible in such a way as to glorify God. Where any church is organized according to external rules without these spiritual gifts it is only a representation of a church, without any animating principle. Gifts are conferred so that the church can edify itself in love (*Eph.* 4:16) and propagate itself in the world.

4. *Both spiritual gifts and saving grace come from Christ's bounty.*

Every grace is a gift, freely bestowed on those who have it (*Matt.* 13:11; *Phil.* 1:29). And although every gift is not saving grace, both gifts and grace proceed from Christ's gracious favour and bounty.

SPIRITUAL GIFTS AND SAVING GRACE: DIFFERENCES

1. *Saving graces are the fruit or fruits of the Spirit (Gal. 5:22; Eph. 5:9; Phil. 1:11).*

As such they proceed from an abiding root or stock, of whose

[174]

nature they partake (*Matt.* 12:33). The Spirit is the true root of these fruits, and he is therefore necessary if fruit is to be borne. He is also the spring in believers, and all saving graces are only the waters rising from the overflowing of that spring (*John* 4:14). He dwells and abides in them for that purpose (*John* 14:17; *Rom.* 8:11; *1 Cor.* 3:16; *John* 15:16). But gifts are not truly fruits of the Spirit, though they are the effects of his working. They proceed from the Spirit's working *on* men, not *in* them and so are of a different nature from saving graces.

2. *Saving grace proceeds from electing love* (*Eph.* 1:3–4; *2 Thess.* 2:13; *Acts* 2:47; 13:48).

Those whom God graciously chooses he prepares for eternal life by communicating the means necessary for that end (*Rom.* 8:28–30). The sonship and salvation of the elect cannot be unless his image is renewed in them in holiness or saving graces. But gifts are only the effects of a temporary election to some office in the church or work in the world. Saul was chosen to be king over the people of God and was given the needed gifts for rule and government. Judas was chosen for a particular work but not given saving grace (*John* 6:70).

3. *Saving grace is an effect of the covenant, and bestowed by virtue of its promises.*

Only those who are made partakers of saving grace are taken into the covenant, but this is not absolutely true of spiritual gifts, though they are connected with the covenant in its outward administration. Saving grace proceeds from the inward essence of the covenant. But the promises of the plentiful pouring out of the Spirit under the new covenant, which often relate to the giving of evangelical gifts, belong to the outward administration of the new covenant rather than to its inward essence.

[175]

4. *Saving grace has an immediate connection with the priestly office of Jesus Christ, but gifts with his kingly office.*
Our reconciliation and peace with God are a direct result of Christ's priestly offering, as is also our sanctification (*Eph.* 5:25–26; *Titus* 2:14). But gifts proceed solely from Christ's office and power as king, and his exaltation to the right hand of God (*Matt.* 28:18; *Acts* 2:33; *Eph.* 4: 7–8, 11–12).

The communication of spiritual gifts, indeed, is a major evidence of the continuance of Christ's mediatorial kingdom. The gifts are *the powers of the new world*, or the age to come, such is their nature and use, the sovereignty seen in their distribution, and the difference between them and all natural endowments.

5. *Saving grace and gifts differ as to their issue, even in this world.*
Gifts may be completely lost or taken away. Those who neglect the talent committed to them will lose their spiritual abilities, so that they will no longer be able to pray, speak or do any other service to the church. 'His right arm shall completely wither, and his right eye shall be totally blinded' (*Zech.* 11:17). These are branches cut off from the vine, or those whose miserable condition is described in Hebrews 6:4–6. But *saving grace* is not like this. Diligence is required if it is to thrive (*2 Pet.* 1:5–10), but its existence and continuance are secured in the covenant of grace.

6. *Saving grace is bestowed first for the good of the one who receives it, but gifts for the benefit of others.*
Grace is the fruit of the special love of God to our souls (*Jer.* 31:3). It is given to renew the image of God in us, to make us like him. Not that it is merely for ourselves: it is meant to give the world an example of the fulfilment of the will of God, to benefit others by its fruits, and to adorn and propagate the doctrine of the gospel in the world. But gifts are primarily

for the benefit of others (*1 Cor.* 12:7), and only in a secondary sense for the good of the one who receives them.

7. *Gifts and grace differ in their nature, operation and effects.*
Gifts, at least those that are resident in us for any length of time, are theoretical rather than practical. They lodge in the mind. Spiritual illumination is what they are based on (*Heb.* 6:4). They do not powerfully change the heart. They may be in those who are unrenewed, and who have nothing in them to preserve them from the worst of sins. But *saving grace* possesses the whole soul. Not only is the mind savingly enlightened, but a principle of spiritual life is infused into the soul, enabling it to obey God. Grace transforms the soul (*Isa.* 11:6–8; *Rom.* 6:17; 12:2; *2 Cor.* 3:18) and inclines it to faith, love and holiness in all things. Gifts do not change the heart or transform the soul into the image of God. Christ may in the end say to those who possessed them, 'I never knew you; depart from me' (*Matt.* 7:23). He will not say this to any whose hearts he has dwelt in.

I will only add that where *grace* and *gifts* are bestowed on the same persons they are very helpful to each other. A soul sanctified by saving grace is the only proper soil for gifts to flourish in. Grace makes a proper use of gifts, prevents their abuse, keeps them from being a matter of pride or contention, and subordinates them in all things to the glory of God. Gifts have a beauty and lustre on them when they are adorned with humility, meekness, reverence for God and compassion for the souls of men. And, in their proper use, gifts stir up grace in our hearts, drawing forth faith, love and delight in God.

3: The Extraordinary Offices of the Church

An office in the church is a special power given by Christ to perform special duties in a special manner, for the edification of the church. These offices have been of two sorts: *extraordinary* and *ordinary*. Four things constituted an extraordinary office in the church: a *call*, *gifts*, *power*, and *employment* out of the ordinary. Thus, apostles, prophets and evangelists were extraordinary officers in the church (*1 Cor.* 12:28; *Eph.* 4:11). We will briefly describe these officers.

APOSTLES

The calling of the apostles was exercised first in subservience to the personal ministry of Jesus Christ. He 'appointed them that they might be with him and that he might send them out to preach' (*Mark* 3:14), initially to the house of Israel only, and then to all nations. Then, secondly, they were to be 'princes in all the earth' (*Psa.* 45:16), rulers and leaders in spiritual things to all the inhabitants of the earth. For this, they received power and commission from Christ himself. Paul, coming later into the office than the eleven, was careful to declare his calling, commission and power to be from Christ directly (*Gal.* 1:1). The apostles' commission involved preaching the gospel in all the world and gathering churches from those that were converted, both Jews and Gentiles. All the spiritual power necessary for this work was given to them.

Another class of temporary officers is seen in the seventy whom Christ sent to go into every city to which he himself would come (*Luke* 10:1–3). In some respects, these were like the evangelists found later in the church. Like them they were subordinate to the apostles in their ministry, and like them they were immediately called by Christ and endued with extraordinary spiritual gifts (*Luke* 10:9, 17, 19).

EVANGELISTS

These were preachers of the gospel distinct from the ordinary teachers of the churches (*Eph.* 4:11; *Acts* 21:8; *2 Tim.* 4:5). They seem to have been called by the apostles by the direction of a spirit of prophecy, or an immediate revelation from Christ. Their work was to preach the gospel, to confirm it with miraculous works, and to settle and perfect those churches whose foundations were laid by the apostles. Although some plead for the continuance of this office in the church, it can be shown that there are no such officers today. No-one today can be called by apostles in response to prophecy or immediate revelation. Nor do any today have the extraordinary spiritual gifts needed for this work.

PROPHETS

There were also prophets with a temporary, extraordinary ministry in the church (*1 Cor.* 12:28; *Eph.* 4:11).The exercise of their ministry is described in Acts 13:1–2. These received immediate revelations and directions from the Spirit (*Acts* 13:2) and foretold things to come by the Spirit's inspiration (*Acts* 11:28–30; 20:22–23; 21:10–11). Sometimes prophecy can be an extraordinary gift without an office (*Acts* 19:6; 21:9). Miracles, healings and tongues are also of this nature. Again, an ordinary office with ordinary gifts can be intended by this term (*Rom.* 12:6), and this continues to be the work and duty of the ordinary teachers of the church.

4: Extraordinary Spiritual Gifts in the Church

We must also consider the extraordinary spiritual gifts with which the church was formerly endowed. Some of these were such as absolutely exceeded the powers and faculties of our minds and souls, such as *miracles* and *healings*. These were the witness of the Holy Spirit to the truth of the gospel (*Heb.* 2:4). But there were also gifts which consisted in extraordinary endowments and improvements of the faculties of men's minds and souls, such as *wisdom, knowledge, utterance* and the like. These differed only in degree from those which are ordinary and continue today. I will consider all these as the apostle enumerates them (*1 Cor.* 12:7–11)

THE WORD OF WISDOM

The 'word of wisdom' denotes wisdom itself, since 'word' often signifies a thing or matter. Our Lord Jesus Christ promised his disciples 'a mouth and wisdom which all your adversaries will not be able to contradict or resist' (*Luke* 21:15). I understand the word of wisdom to be a peculiar spiritual skill and ability for the wise management of the gospel for the furtherance of the truth, especially in defending it against adversaries. Insofar as this gift is continued today, we may be guided in obtaining and exercising it by *a sense of our own insufficiency* for anything requiring wisdom (*2 Cor.* 2:16; *1 Cor.* 3:18), *earnest prayer* for a supply of this wisdom (*James* 1:5), due *meditation on our great pattern*, the Lord Jesus Christ, *avoidance of self-confidence, hastiness and rashness*, and a *seeking of humility, meekness, patience and bold constancy in profession*.

THE WORD OF KNOWLEDGE

This signifies knowledge itself, or it may be the expression of knowledge in words. I understand this gift to be a peculiar and special insight into the mysteries of the gospel, enabling those who received it to teach and instruct others. Those who first dispensed the gospel were particularly skilled in this (*Acts* 20:27; *Eph.* 3:8–9; *Col.* 4:2–4). Although no-one today receives knowledge by immediate revelation, the ministers of the church still receive a sufficient measure of knowledge for the edification of the church.

FAITH

This does not mean the saving grace of faith, which is common to all believers. Some take it to be the faith which can perform miracles (*1 Cor.* 13:2), but because healings and the working of miracles are mentioned next, I rather take it to be a peculiar confidence, boldness and assurance of mind in the profession of the gospel and the administration of its ordinances. It is that 'boldness in the faith' referred to by the apostle (*1 Tim.* 3:13). This is a most excellent gift for all occasions, and sometimes its presence in one individual has preserved a whole church from coldness or backsliding, as in the case of Luther. It is a fearful thing when in times of trial this gift is withheld and cowardice and carnal wisdom take its place.

GIFTS OF HEALING

This gift involved the sudden and miraculous recovery of the sick through the laying on of hands, in the name of the Lord Jesus. The Acts of the Apostles gives many instances (*Acts* 3:7; 5:15; 9:33–34; 19:12). Why is this gift mentioned separately from the working of miracles? This seems to be done because healing was a sign to those who believe, in token that the kingdom of God had come, and that Christ had borne and taken away sin, the root cause of disease and sickness, whereas the working of miracles was a sign to those who did not believe, as tongues were (*1 Cor.* 14:22), and served for their conviction. Healing also has a peculiar goodness, relief and kindness towards mankind in it, which other miraculous works do not share. So it particularly showed the goodness, love and compassion of Christ, the Author of the gospel. It was also accompanied with some outward signs, such as laying on of hands or anointing with oil, which other miracles were not. It was therefore reckoned as a distinct gift by itself.

THE WORKING OF MIRACLES

A miracle is an immediate effect of divine power, exceeding all created abilities. Every miracle was accompanied by a peculiar act of faith, sometimes called 'the faith of miracles' (*1 Cor.* 13:2) and had an immediate revelation for its warrant. Those who had this kind of faith could not work miracles when, where and how they pleased, but only when the Spirit infallibly showed them what he would do. This gift was exceedingly useful for the propagation of the gospel (see *Acts* 2:6; 14:11). It gained a hearing for the gospel and authenticated the preachers of it as sent from God. It also confirmed and established those who were weak in the faith or newly converted.

PROPHECY

I take this in its largest sense, both as a faculty of prediction and as an ability to declare the mind of God from the Word by the immediate revelation of the Holy Spirit. It had a double use: the conviction and conversion of such as came into their church assemblies, and the exposition and application of the Word by an extraordinary assistance of the Spirit of God. The manner of the exercise of this gift was limited and regulated by the apostle (*1 Cor.* 14:29–33) to ensure peace and order and to allow what was said to be judged by others, so that edification might follow.

DISCERNING OF SPIRITS

When God granted to the church the privilege of the immediate revelation of his will, Satan stirred up others to lay claim to the same spirit of prophecy for his own malicious purposes. What was offered *doctrinally* was to be tried by the written Word (*Isa.* 8:20), but in addition God granted this gift so that the *spirits* that men claimed to act by might be rightly judged. When spiritual gifts abounded, so did false claims to such gifts. Now it is sufficient for our preservation in the truth that the infallible rule of the Word and the ordinary assistance of the Spirit should guide us.

TONGUES AND THEIR INTERPRETATION

The gift of tongues (*Acts* 2:4) was a visible pledge of the enduing of the apostles with power from above (*Acts* 1:8). By it God signified that the grace and mercy of the covenant was no longer confined to one nation or language, and that he would bring in his kingdom, not by force but by the preaching of the Word, through the light and efficacy of the Spirit of God. This gift was afterwards very much diffused among those who believed (*Acts* 10:46; 19:6; *1 Cor.* 14:22). It was generally used to express praise to God for his wonderful works of grace. In the assemblies of the church it was of little use unless for the conviction of unbelievers who came in (*1 Cor.* 14:1–27).

5: How Spiritual Gifts Promote Christ's Kingdom

These extraordinary spiritual gifts which were abundantly poured out (*Acts* 2:33) were evidences of the exaltation of Christ and of his acceptance with God. By them the Spirit convicted the world of sin, of righteousness and of judgment (*John* 16:8–11), and by them the exalted Christ carried on his work among men.

There was no definite limited time after which they were to cease. Those peculiar to the apostles spanned their lifetime. After that, no-one had the apostolic office, power, or gifts. The same is true of the evangelists. And we have no undoubted evidence that any of the truly miraculous gifts were given to anyone after the generation which had known Christ in the flesh or received the Holy Spirit by the ministry of those who had. It is not unlikely that God put forth miraculous power at times during a longer period. He may do so still. But the superstition and folly of some subsequent ages, inventing countless false and foolish miracles, only raised prejudice against the gospel and allowed Satan to impose endless delusions on Christians.

However, although all these gifts and miraculous workings ceased, some absolutely, some as to the way they were communicated or exercised, something analogous to them was continued. As well as the extraordinary officers, the exalted Christ gave *pastors and teachers* and equipped them with all that was needed for the edification of the church. The gifts and graces still given, together with grace and real holiness, are the true glory, honour and beauty of the church in any age. And the way to promote the true unity of the church is for all

Christians to return to those things in which the life and spirit of the early church consisted.

THE SPIRITUAL POWERS OF THE GOSPEL

As we have said, these spiritual gifts are called 'the powers of the age to come' (*Heb.* 6:5), that is, the effectual principles and operations which characterize the kingdom of Christ and govern the way in which it is set up, advanced and propagated in the world. I will briefly attempt to show how these extraordinary gifts were the spiritual powers of the gospel, to the exclusion of the wisdom, skill, power and authority of men, and afterwards I will try to show how the more ordinary gifts of the Spirit are to be the means by which the gospel and the church are continued and preserved in the world.

THE ENABLING OF CHRIST'S SERVANTS

The men Christ chose and called for this work were subject to all possible disadvantages. They were uneducated and untrained (*Acts* 4:13). They were poor and of no reputation in the world. In many cases they seem to have been fearful and lacking in firmness and conviction. These disadvantages were all removed by the imparting of spiritual gifts of supernatural wisdom, power and boldness. In the strength of these spiritual abilities, and not with force, arms or carnal power, they went forth against the kingdom of Satan and of darkness, contended with the gates of hell, and overcame both the wisdom of the Greeks and the religion of the Jews.

THE POWER OF PREACHING

The preaching of the Word, the sword of the Spirit, was the great instrument these men used. What had been foolish and despicable to those to whom it was preached (*1 Cor.* 1:18) then obtained authority over the minds of men (*1 Cor.* 2:4–5). Without any arts of oratory or studied eloquence, the Word came to be the arrows of Christ which were sharp in the hearts of men (see *Psa.* 45:5). So the apostle describes the success of these administrations as an absolute conquest in which all opposition was broken, all fortifications demolished, and complete obedience secured (*2 Cor.* 10:4–5). And this was achieved by virtue of the spiritual gifts which the Lord Christ made to be the powers of his kingdom.

THE SENSE OF DIVINE POWER

Those gifts which consisted in miraculous operations filled the world with an apprehension of a divine power accompanying the Word and the preachers of it. This was necessary to awaken the world from its stupor and security, its contentment in idolatry and sin, and the ingrained prejudice which possessed the minds of men. Miraculous gifts were also very useful in removing the scandal of the cross. Christ crucified was a stumbling block to the Jews and foolishness to the Greeks. But when this weakness and folly was obviously owned by God and witnessed to by the manifest effects of divine power, a way was made for the entrance of the Word into the minds and consciences of men.

These instances show how spiritual gifts were the weapons that the Lord Christ made use of to subdue the world, destroy the kingdom of Satan, and establish his own church on the earth. His use of them is a glorious evidence of his divine power and wisdom.

6: The Continuance of the Ministry

Those spiritual gifts which we call ordinary, to distinguish them from those which utterly exceeded the powers and faculties of men, continue in the church till now, and will till the consummation of all things. But before we deal with them particularly, we must speak of a prior gift of Christ to which they relate, *the ministry*, as its nature is illustrated in Ephesians 4:7–16.

There is no other single passage of Scripture in which the institution, purpose and benefit of the ministry are so clearly declared.

A GIFT OF CHRIST

The ministry is declared to be *a gift of Christ* (*Eph.* 4:11). If this were not so, it would not have been lawful for men to institute such an office or appoint men to fill it. He had long promised to give such a gift (*Psa.* 68:18; *Jer.* 3:15). His doing so is an act of his mediatorial power (*Matt.* 28:18) and a fruit of his love and care (*1 Cor.* 12:28). It follows that all offices in the church which are not of Christ's institution are set up in defiance of his authority and contempt of his care.

The ministry was instituted from Christ's ascended glory (*Eph.* 4:8). Words describing the glorious appearance of God on Mount Sinai are here applied to Christ in his ascension. The greatness and eminence of the gift imparted is seen in the grandeur of its introduction, in the humiliation which preceded it (verse 9), in the glorious qualification of Christ to impart it (verses 8 and 10), in the nature and value of the gift itself, and in the variety and diversity of the offices and officers which Christ gave, both for the foundation and for the subsequent building up of the church. As to this latter requirement, the only ordinary officers that Christ has given are *pastors* and *teachers*. He gave these as a standing ordinance and institution, and continues their office by giving spiritual gifts and abilities to men to enable them to carry out the work. He has also given power to his church in all ages to call and separate to the work such men as he has fitted and gifted for it. And the rules by which these things are to be done are all laid down in the Word.

THE PURPOSE OF THE GIFT

The purpose of this gift of the ministry is expressed both positively (*Eph.* 4:12) and negatively (*Eph.* 4:14). Positively, the ministry is ordained for the good and advantage of the church, in the gathering of the saints into complete church order and their edification as the body of Christ, until they come to complete conformity to and enjoyment of him. Negatively, the ministry is to protect the church from being deceived by false doctrine, errors and heresies, and by delivering the saints out of a childlike state, characterized by weakness, instability and wilfulness. As the ministry is always to continue in the church (verse 13), it remains the great means of influencing the whole church to a proper discharge of its duty, so that it may be edified in love (verses 15–16).

Those who are called to this office must labour to approve themselves as a gift of Christ by endeavouring to be furnished with gracious qualifications, useful endowments, diligent labour and exemplary conduct, showing love, meekness, self-denial and readiness to take up the cross.

7: Spiritual Gifts Granted to the Ministry

What we will now seek to establish is that *there is a special work of the Holy Spirit in providing able ministers of the New Testament for the edification of the church,* and that *he does communicate spiritual gifts to men for this purpose,* without which they have no right to be considered ministers.

THE PROMISE OF CHRIST

The Lord Jesus Christ has faithfully promised to be with his church to the end of the age (*Matt.* 28:20; *Rev.* 21:3). It is his temple and his tabernacle in which he dwells and walks continually. And it is this presence of Christ which makes the church to be what it is.

Correct outward order is no evidence of the presence of Christ, for his promised presence is by his Spirit. We do not refer here to the essential presence of Christ in his divine nature, nor yet his human nature, for we know that we are not to expect his return till his coming in judgment (*Acts* 1:11; 3:21). But his promise to be present with his church was to be fulfilled by the sending of the Spirit in his place to do for them all that he had not yet done (*John* 14:16–18, 26–28; 15:26; 16:7–15).

This presence of the Spirit is secured to the church by an everlasting covenant (*Isa.* 59:20–21), a part of the covenant that God has made in Christ the Redeemer. Without the performance of this, it would not *be* the church, for the gospel is called the ministration of the Spirit (*2 Cor.* 3:8) and the ministers of the gospel, the ministers of the Spirit. Now this description must refer to the peculiar assistance of the Spirit by which they are enabled to administer the gospel and its worship, or to the fact that it is by the ministry of the gospel that the Spirit is administered and communicated to the disciples of Christ (see *Gal.* 3:2). In either sense, what we are contending for is confirmed, that the Spirit and his special operations continue in the church for ever.

THE PURPOSE OF THE PROMISE

The great purpose for which the Spirit is thus promised is the continuance and preservation of the church in the world. Christ's kingdom in the world is to last 'throughout all generations'(*Psa.* 72:5; *Isa.* 9:7). The gates of hell shall not prevail against it (*Matt.* 16:18). This cannot be accomplished by the work or will of man, but only through the promise of the Spirit. The very being of the church, in its internal union with Christ, its living Head, depends on the Spirit, and if men are not furnished with the gifts of the Spirit, all true gospel administrations become impossible.

SPIRITUAL GIFTS IMPARTED TO THE MINISTRY

Various places in Scripture assert the imparting of such gifts to the ordinary ministry of the church in all ages. The parable of the talents (*Matt.* 25:14–30) speaks of this very thing. The talents in the parable are abilities to trade which Christ, as Head and King of the church, gives to those who are employed under him in the service of his house and the work of the gospel. Wherever there is a ministry which Christ sets up, appoints or owns, he furnishes all those whom he employs with gifts and abilities suitable to their work, and he does this by the Spirit. Where there are no such gifts, there is no ministry that he either accepts or approves.

[190]

A second testimony to the same thing is found in Romans 12:4–8. The apostle is plainly speaking of the ordinary state of the church after its foundation, so that what he describes is necessary in all ages and conditions. Everything in the church depends on this principle, that 'to each one of us grace [is] given according to the measure of Christ's gift' (*Eph.* 4:7). The whole duty of anyone in the church is that he act according to the gift that he has been made partaker of (*Rom.* 12:6). Parallel testimonies include 1 Peter 4:10–11 and Ephesians 4:7–16. In this whole discussion it should be remembered that we are speaking of spiritual gifts which are neither purely natural endowments nor attainable by our own industry and diligence.

Just as these gifts are absolutely necessary to the ministration of the gospel, so the neglect and subsequent loss of them led to the apostasy of the Christian church, as regards its outward profession. It could not be otherwise, for the visible profession of the church depends on the reception and use of spiritual gifts. And the example of the church of Rome shows us what endless human inventions will be resorted to when, through the loss of spiritual gifts, spiritual ministrations are also lost.

On this point, I would appeal, finally, to experience. In our own day the Spirit continues to dispense spiritual gifts in great variety to gospel ministers who are called to their office according to his mind and will. Do they not find, when they humbly inquire into these things in the fear of God, that by the assistance of the Spirit the Word is made mighty through them, for all the purposes for which it is sent? And where the gifts of the Spirit are excluded, so is all true edification, and all the real concerns of the gospel.

8: The Gifts of the Spirit for Doctrine, Worship and Discipline

F inally, we are to consider how the Spirit of God equips the ministry with the gifts necessary for teaching, the ordering of worship, and discipline in the church. While it may not be possible for us to enumerate all the gifts which the Spirit endows ministers with, we will speak of those most necessary for these three matters.

DOCTRINE

Teaching is the principal work of the ministry. The apostles gave themselves to it in a special way (*Acts* 6:4). Hence all ministers of the gospel are to take particular heed to it (*1 Tim.* 1:3; 4:13, 16; 5:17; *2 Tim.* 4:1–3). With respect to this work, there are three spiritual gifts which must be considered:

1. *Wisdom, knowledge or understanding* in the mysteries of the gospel. Though these things may be distinguished, I put them together because they all refer to that acquaintance with and comprehension of the doctrine of the gospel which is absolutely necessary for all who are called to preach. This is not so easily acquired as some think. The apostle speaks of his 'knowledge in the mystery of Christ' (*Eph.* 3:4). To be wise in the understanding of this mystery (see *Eph.* 1:8–9; 3:3–6, 18, 19; *Col.* 4:3) ministers must seek wisdom from God (*James* 1:5). The Spirit, in particular, gives the 'word of wisdom' (*1 Cor.* 12:8), and it is the first ministerial gift he bestows on any.

2. *An ability to divide the Word rightly* (*2 Tim.* 2:15). This too is a particular gift of the Holy Spirit. Ministers are stewards in the house of God and must give a portion to all the servants that

are in the house, according to their needs, and according to the will of their Lord and Master (*Luke* 21:42–43). This requires a sound judgment concerning the state of those ministered to, a knowledge of the work of God's grace in the minds and hearts of men, and an acquaintance with spiritual temptations and difficulties, and spiritual diseases and their cures.

3. *The gift of utterance.* This is particularly reckoned by the apostle among the gifts of the Spirit (*1 Cor.* 1:5; *2 Cor.* 8:7). The nature of it is 'opening the mouth boldly to make known the mystery of the gospel' (*Eph.* 6:19). It should not be confused with natural volubility, but involves a freedom or enlargement to declare the truth, boldness and holy confidence, a gravity becoming the majesty of Christ and his gospel, and an authority which accompanies the delivery of the Word.

THE WORSHIP OF GOD

The various acts of worship are all comprised in *prayer*, by which I understand all the confessions, supplications, thanksgivings and praises made to God in the church. These do not depend on the natural abilities of men, but on the help of the Spirit of God. And this consists in a special spiritual gift bestowed on men for this purpose. I will not enlarge on this here, since I have spoken of it in Part 3 of the present book, but I will only add here that those who lack this gift are not equipped to undertake the office of the ministry.

DISCIPLINE

God has established rule or discipline in the church (*Rom.* 12:8; *1 Cor.* 12:28; *1 Tim.* 5:17; *1 Thess.* 5:12; *Heb.* 13:7, 17), and has made the ministers of the church its guides, rulers and overseers. But this rule is spiritual and has nothing in common with the exercise of power in the world. Christ forbade his disciples to rule after the manner of the Gentiles (*Matt.* 20:25–28). Those who ruled were to serve others in love and apply the Word of God to them in a humble, holy and spiritual way. All the power they had was for edification (*2 Cor.* 10:8). Whatever rule is exercised in the church to other ends is foreign to the gospel and tends to the destruction of the church itself.

This being so, it is impossible to exercise rule aright without the special help of the Spirit of God. Can any man claim to know the mind of Christ concerning all the needs of the church, and administer the power of Christ in these matters? Therefore the apostle teaches that wisdom, skill and understanding to a minister the rule of Christ in the church to its edification, with faithfulness and diligence, is a special gift of the Spirit (*Rom.* 12:8; *1 Cor.* 12:28). It is the Holy Spirit who makes men overseers to shepherd the flock of God (*Acts* 20:28), and what he calls them to, he will certainly equip them for.

SPIRITUAL GIFTS IMPARTED TO ALL BELIEVERS

The Holy Spirit continues to impart spiritual gifts to all members of the church in a great variety of degrees, according to their circumstances, to their own edification, and the good of the church. These do not differ in their nature from those given to ministers, though ministers must excel in them, as going before the whole church in the exercise of them. The Spirit quickens and animates the whole body of the church and all the members of it, uniting them to Christ (*1 Cor.* 12:12–13). As the administrator of all supernatural gifts, he furnishes the whole body and all its members with spiritual abilities, for its edification (*Eph.* 4:15–16; *Col.* 2:19; *1 Cor.* 12:12–20).

All believers grow in grace by the exercise of their own gifts in spiritual duties. Every individual stands in need of some such gifts on his own account, and most because of duties to others, such as their families. In the church, every member has some place in the body which requires a spiritual gift, as an eye, a hand, a foot (*1 Cor.* 12:15–20), and supplies are communicated to the whole body from the Head (*Eph.* 4:15–16; *Col.* 2:19). All should exercise the abilities given to them, keeping within the measure they have received.

SEEKING SPIRITUAL GIFTS

How may we come to partake of spiritual gifts? I would observe that they are not now imparted by a sudden extraordinary outpouring, as were the gifts of miracles and tongues. That dispensation of the Spirit has long since ceased, and where it is claimed it may well be suspected as a fanatical delusion, for, just as the reason for these gifts, which exceed all our own powers, has ceased, so also has the communication of them, and the manner in which they were conveyed too.

But I would add that the infusion of spiritual light into the mind, and the gifts that follow from it, may well be sudden, or take only a short time to accomplish. It should be remembered that spiritual gifts are not strictly obtainable by our own diligence, without submission to the sovereign will and pleasure of the Holy Spirit. However, they are usually both attained and increased, as is grace itself, in the use of the right means. And a brief review of these means will bring us to the end of this discussion.

The first means is a preparation of the soul in *humility, meekness and teachableness*. The Spirit is not likely to impart his gifts to proud, self-conceited men, vainly puffed up in their fleshly minds. I need hardly add that those who despise all these gifts are not likely to receive them. The second means is *prayer*. The apostle directs us to this when

[195]

tells us to desire these gifts earnestly (*1 Cor.* 12:31). The third is *diligence in study of and meditation on the Word of God.* The fourth is *faithful use of what we receive.* Trading is the only way to increase our talents, and exercise develops our gifts.

And finally, our natural endowments of speech, memory, judgment and the like, developed by reading, learning and diligent study, enhance and beautify these gifts, where they have been received.

Other titles in this series of Owen abridgements:

THE HOLY SPIRIT

'Owen on the Holy Spirit', as this work has been known to generations of Christians, is without question one of the truly great Christian books. Originally published in 1674 as *Pneumatologia, or, A Discourse concerning the Holy Spirit*, it is a massive work, taking up 650 pages in the Banner of Truth edition of Owen's *Works* (Volume 3). This abridged version prepared by Dr R. J. K. Law will help modern readers to get to grips with Owen.

'An admirable effort at making this great 17th century Puritan theologian and teacher more accessible to the Christian reading public.'

NEW LIFE

ISBN: 978 0 85151 698 1, 216 pp. Paperback

THE GLORY OF CHRIST

This abridgement of John Owen's work *The Glory of Christ* shows him at his richest and most mature as he expounds the heart of the gospel with biblical insight and understanding. Owen speaks to our own generation from his nearness to eternity and teaches us how to see Christ more clearly and serve him more faithfully.

'This is a book to warm the heart as well as instruct the mind.'

AUSTRALIAN PRESBYTERIAN

ISBN: 978 0 85151 661 5, 184 pp. Paperback

COMMUNION WITH GOD

John Owen believed that communion with God lay at the heart of the Christian life. He never lost the sense of amazement expressed by John: 'Our fellowship is with the Father and with his Son, Jesus Christ.' The original work was written in a day like our own when the Christian faith was being reduced either to rationalism or to mysticism. Owen's exposition is presented here in an abridged and modernized form by Dr R. J. K. Law.

'A delight to read . . . as [Owen] beautifully and personally applies Scripture.'

REFORMED THEOLOGICAL JOURNAL

ISBN: 978 0 85151 607 3, 224 pp. Paperback

APOSTASY FROM THE GOSPEL

The idea that professing Christians may prove not to be true Christians is a deeply disturbing one, but this is not a reason to avoid the issue. This modernized abridgement of Owen's work by Dr R. J. K. Law makes its powerful teaching readily accessible to modern readers. It is a work which wounds in order to heal.

'A masterpiece of spiritual penetration and insight.'

FREE CHURCH MONTHLY RECORD

ISBN: 978 0 85151 609 7, 184 pp. Paperback

THE BANNER OF TRUTH TRUST

3 Murrayfield Road   P O Box 621, Carlisle
Edinburgh EH12 6EL   Philadelphia 17013
UK   USA

banneroftruth.org